A Christian Reads
the Qur'an

Honest Reading
Honest Reflection

James Wright

New Yurt Books

New Yurt Books

Committed to quality research and writing
across boundaries of language and culture.
For more information or to order this book in larger quantities at reduced cost
please email: info@christianreadsquran.com
www.christianreadsquran.com

ISBN-13: 978-1984937933

ISBN-10: 1984937936

DEDICATION

In memory of the teacher Nabeel Qureshi and for all who sincerely seek the Truth. As Francis Schaeffer often said, those who ask honest questions deserve honest answers.

CONTENTS

A Christian Reads the Qur'an

ACKNOWLEDGMENTS

My wife used to say she wished she had married a farmer. I'm not and she didn't, at least not in the literal sense. But whether sitting at a keyboard or in a tractor, the writer and farmer both face the huge job of trying to prepare their soil so new seeds can take root, grow and produce a harvest. Waiting patiently during long hours of my writing, she not only offered encouragement, but always did it with her unique flare that brings color to life. I also want to thank the many friends who gave their precious time and energy proofreading the book so it could reach a higher quality. They suggested changes in style and substance that have made it far better than anything I could have done alone.

Reading in Ramadan

This Ramadan I decided to read the Qur'an. Over the years I have studied the Qur'an, but this time I wanted to read the entire Qur'an *very carefully*.

I follow Isa al-Masih. Sometimes people call me a Christian, though I've learned that many do not really understand the word and sometimes have wrong or really strange ideas about Christians. I live in Asia, but it doesn't matter what part of the world I visit. It could be frozen Moscow in the far north or the steamy jungles of Thailand to the south. Many think Christian means European or American and no more. It's someone who drinks lots of alcohol, eats pork and perhaps even chases prostitutes. Or worse yet, they figure it's quite likely some Christians are prostitutes.

Movies and television feed these mistaken ideas. Isn't a church a beautiful old building where sinners confess shocking sins to the priest? After confession everything goes back to normal so the unchaste people can do more shocking things like get drunk and eat loads of pork together.

The whole picture really is quite repulsive to me and if that is genuine

Christian faith, I say toss it all in the bottom of the ocean.

I'm not that kind of Christian. Is an immoral person even a Christian? As we will see in this book, that's not the way of Allah. Drunkenness is obviously bad and gets people into all sorts of trouble. I don't think eating pork in itself is necessarily wrong, but I respect people who don't eat it. You will never see me eat a cat or dog. I believe in marriage between one man and one woman and like Allah teaches, I reject sexual immorality because it degrades and destroys lives. We are created for love that endures, not lust that abuses.

Miriam's[1] son Isa has a special title. *Al-Masih*. His followers are called *Masihi* or Christians. They love, trust and follow him in a holy life that is very different from the way of the world.

In the month of Ramadan my neighbors faithfully fast. Sunset brings lights at the mosques, gunshots, Iftar soup, piping hot flat bread and piles of rice pilaf. After everyone fills their empty stomachs they relax in the soft afterglow of the feast and sip endless cups of hot tea and coffee.

Long, hot days make summer the hardest time for Ramadan. The strictest fast prohibits water, cigarettes and a person's own spittle. So hard! Yet Muslims continue to fast year after year, hoping to make themselves better slaves of Allah.

Millions of people around the world live immersed in Islamic communities. My Muslim friends and neighbors are curious to meet a non-Muslim. They ask me, "What do you think about the prophet Muhammad?" When I say that I've read the Qur'an they eagerly ask,

---

[1] Miriam=Mary. For most names I use the Arabic forms. However in the quotations from the Tawrat, Prophets and Injil the English forms appear in their original spellings. Yusuf Ali also uses English forms in his interpretive translation of the Qur'an. From this point I will leave the reader to identify what English name goes with the Arabic form.

"What kind of effect did it have on you? What do you think about it?"

My ancestors were probably not Arabs, but who knows for sure? Long ago my ancestors migrated from remote places. Genetic tests confirm my father's fathers lived in Spain, Ireland, Norway and even the Caucasus of Central Asia. Like every human, they descended from Adam and Hawwa. I speak Turkish, English, Kazakh and a little Russian, but only have an introduction to Arabic.

Many Muslims would say that to really understand the Qur'an, I need to understand Qur'anic Arabic. But just a small percentage of people on earth can read and speak modern Arabic, much less the Arabic of the Qur'an. Furthermore, the first copies of the Qur'an used Arabic letters with no vowel markings, so no one today knows exactly how the first Muslims pronounced the words.

The Arabic language and I have a polite relationship, but we aren't best friends. I have to study the Qur'anic Arabic with the help of interpretations as well as a transliteration of the Arabic in Latin script.

Islamic scholars say that Qur'anic Arabic is a divine language and cannot be translated. Mustafa Kemal Ataturk urged mosques to give the call to prayer in Turkish, but this was later considered unacceptable. Wherever the Qur'an is recited, it must be in the original Qur'anic Arabic, even if some of the hearers cannot understand the precise meaning.

To study the Qur'an, I purchased an English interpretation called *The Meaning of the Holy Qur'an* by Abdullah Yusuf 'Ali. I used several Turkish interpretation online. Sometimes the interpretations are similar to one another, but other times not. None of them take the place of learning Arabic. Unfortunately, most people don't live long enough to successfully accomplish such a huge task.

Why would a Christian read the Qur'an? To criticize it? To convert to Islam? Many of my Muslim friends want me to read it because they believe it is the most important book in the world.

I don't want to criticize the Qur'an. I do want to be thoughtful, wise, humble and prayerful. Do I want to become a Muslim? I want to know and follow the Truth, wherever I find it. My destiny isn't determined by my race or culture or parents or fate. What if I have a choice? If I can choose the truth, I want to decide after seeking it with my whole heart.

My purpose is also to look for respect. Far too often Muslims and Christians live in parallel universes. Reading the Qur'an can help build bridges of respect between one other. The Qur'an says "do not argue with the People of the Book except in the best way" (Surah 29:46 Al-Ankabut).

> Many of my Muslim friends want me to read the Qur'an because they believe it is the most important book in the world.

When the Qur'an talks about earlier books sent by Allah it usually refers to some or all of the Tawrat, Prophets (including Zabur) and Injil.[2] I have studied the Tawrat, Prophets and Injil I'm curious to see why the Qur'an also talks about these important subjects: the Creator, creation, good and evil, angels and demons, Heaven and Hell, prophets, the *Tawrat, Zabur, Injil* and Isa al-Masih. These things are important to me. They are important to Muslims too.

---

[2] I sometimes refer to the Tawrat, Prophets and Injil as the *Earlier Books*.

Tawrat = First 5 books of Musa

Prophets = Holy writings before Isa al-Masih, including Zabur containing Davud's songs

Injil = Good News about Isa al-Masih, the Kalimatullah (Word of Allah)

Chapter 1

Surah 1: Al Fatihah (The Opening)

Where to begin? The Qur'an is not a small book. Neither is it an easy book. The language is complex and so is the content. There are over 6000 Ayat in 114 Surahs. In 650 CE Muslims wrote out the first copies of the Qur'an in complete form. Later more and more copies were written until today, with the help of modern printing presses and digital technology, there are billions of copies of the Qur'an in the world. The number keeps growing every year as Islam grows.

Copies of the Qur'an are printed with ink and paper. Still, many people believe that since the ink and paper represent Allah's eternal words dictated to Muhammad from the angel Jibril, the ink and paper should be handled reverently. To disrespect the physical book is to disrespect Allah. No Muslim would ever allow a Qur'an to touch the ground.

I could attempt to read through the Qur'an in one of three basic ways. The first way is to read straight through, from beginning to end. Another way is to read according to topics like Paradise and Hell or prophets and angels. A third way is to read through the Qur'an chronologically, starting with the Surahs that first came to Muhammad and then following them in order to the last one given at the end of his life. But that is more complicated.

The simplest way to read the Qur'an is to begin in the beginning. Surah 1, Al Fatihah.

> In the name of Allah, Most Gracious, Most Merciful.
> Praise be to Allah, The Cherisher and Sustainer of the Worlds;
> Most Gracious, Most Merciful;
> Master of the Day of Judgment.
> Thee do we worship, and Thine aid we seek.
> Show us the straight way,
> The way of those on whom Thou hast bestowed Thy Grace, those whose (portion) is not wrath, and who go not astray.

Billions of times a day, the words of Surah 1:1 fall off the lips of Muslims around the world. Bismillah Al Rahman, Rahim. Those words sound ancient. They also sound familiar. Looking back 2000 years before Muhammad, I discovered these words in the Tawrat, "for the Lord[3] your God[4] is *gracious and merciful.*"[5] And, "the Lord...show you *mercy*, and have *compassion* upon you."[6]

The Hebrew language in the Tawrat is very close to the Qur'anic Arabic. After all, both languages come from the children of Ibrahim. Just look at these words.

---

[3] "Lord", sometimes spelled "LORD", in the Tawrat and Prophets (including Zabur) is often used for the word YHWH (יהוה), the holy name of Allah that means "I am who I am."

[4] In the quotations from the Tawrat, Prophets and Injil I leave the original word "God." In my comments I mostly use the word "Allah."

[5] Prophets, 2 Chronicles 30:9

[6] Tawrat, Deuteronomy 13:17

רָחַם *Racham*, compassionate/ الرَّحْمَٰنِ al-Raḥmāni, gracious

חַנּוּן *Channun*, gracious

רַחוּם *Rachum*, merciful/ الرَّحِيم al-Raḥīmi, merciful

These aren't the only Ayat that call Allah gracious and merciful. In the Tawrat and Prophets, *Rachum* is found 47 times, *Racham* 44 times and *Channun* 13 times. Over and over the ancient prophets uttered these holy words. The Qur'an also has 123 Ayat that call Allah merciful and 62 Ayat calling him gracious.

Surah 1 praises Allah and offers a prayer. "Show us the straight way." If we need Allah's help finding the straight way, where are the crooked ways? How many crooked ways are there? Where did the crooked ways come from? Where do they go, is it to Hell?

The Straight Way must be hard to find. If it were easy to find we wouldn't need Allah's help to find it. Left to ourselves we have little hope of avoiding a wide road that leads to destruction. Something is causing people big problems. Surah 1 acknowledges that not all paths are the same. So how do we recognize the Straight Way? This must be one of the most important questions we face.

Chapter 2

Surah 2: Al Baqarah (The Heifer)

Some weeks after Ramadan my neighbors slaughtered a large bull behind the house for *Eid al Adha* (Holiday of Sacrifice). Prayers went heavenward and blood flowed out from the jugular veins of countless animals.

Surah 2 is simply called Al Baqarah (The Heifer). I thought of my neighbors' dying bull as I studied Surah 2. It has 286 Ayat, making it the longest in the Qur'an. Because it is so long, I can't respond to every Ayat, but it deserves careful reading.

Proof of Muhammad's Prophethood (Surah 2:23-24)

Ayat 23 and 24 give what is considered the ultimate proof of Muhammad's prophethood: his Arabic recitation was believed to be far superior to anyone else. His amazing and powerful oratory skills seemed so far superior to those of anyone else, his followers took it as sure proof that his message came from Allah.

The Rise and Fall of Humans (Surah 2:30-34)

Al Baqarah explains human creation in Ayat 30-34. Interestingly, it says the angels anticipated a very big problem. Humans would rebel.

> Behold, Thy Lord said to the angels: "I will create a vice-regent on earth." They said: "Wilt Thou place therein one who will make mischief therein and shed blood?

In spite of future human rebellion, Ayat 34 says Allah decided not only to create humans but told the angels to bow down before them.

The Zabur agrees that it seems strange Allah would express interest in humanity. Davud wrote,

> What is mankind that you are mindful of them, human beings that you care for them? You have made them a little lower than the angels and crowned them with glory and honor. You made them rulers over the works of your hands; you put everything under their feet.[7]

After Allah creates Adam and his wife Hawwa, they enjoy a beautiful garden where they can enjoy fruit from every tree except one. But then Satan comes and deceives them so they eat the forbidden fruit. The Qur'an says, "Then did Satan make them slip from the… and get them out of the state in which they had been." What was their state of existence before they took the forbidden fruit? Was it not a state of innocence, with no guilt, shame, or condemnation? When they lost their innocence, Allah sent them out of the garden with no return.

Allah Promises Help

Adam and Hawwa needed right guidance and so do all their descendants. But there is another problem. What about the guilt of breaking Allah's laws? Imagine someone steals $100,000 from a bank. Eventually the police catch the thief. He tells them he has found the Straight Way and so he wants to give $50,000 to an orphanage and

---

[7] Zabur 8:5

return the rest. He promises them he will never steal again. Will his good deeds and repentance completely erase his debt and take his guilt? What if he had killed the bank guard when he robbed the bank?

The Tawrat describes Allah's warning to Adam and Hawwa about the forbidden fruit. Allah told them that if they ate the fruit they would surely die.

Satan is a liar. He lied to Hawwa and said that they would not die if they ate the forbidden fruit. But they did die. First, they eventually got old and sick and died a physical death. Second, and more importantly, their relationship with Allah died. They became ashamed of their sin and tried to hide from Allah.

Yet something amazing happened. First, Allah promised to send a very special person he called a "Seed." Allah warned Satan, "I will put enmity between thee and the woman, and between thy seed and her seed; it shall bruise thy head, and thou shalt bruise his heel."[8] Who could crush Satan?

Second, Allah made the first sacrifice in human history. Instead of leaving them in their shameful nakedness, Allah himself clothed Adam and Hawwa in animal skins. Where did these clothes of skin come from? Allah himself killed the sacrificial animals to cover their nakedness and shame. Only he could provide the satisfactory sacrifice to cover their shame.

Truth or Falsehood (Surah 2:42)

The Roman governor once asked Isa, "What is truth?" The Qur'an warns against covering truth with falsehood. Knowing truth brings freedom. A man who discovers he has a damaged valve in his heart must face a painful surgery, but knowing the truth can lead him to a

---

[8] Tawrat, Genesis 3:15

longer and happier life.

How do we know the truth?

Science and technology do amazing things. Airplanes can circle the world in hours. Computers connect people across countries and translate languages instantly. Medicines and vaccines extend human life. But none of these can fully tell us Allah's spiritual truth. He exists apart from our material universe.

The Injil says, "Test everything, hold fast to that which is good."[9] In modern terms this is called critical thinking. It means that asking whether something is true or not can help lead us in the discovery of truth. It looks for multiple kinds of evidence.

> Allah himself clothed Adam and Hawwa in animal skins...only he could provide the satisfactory sacrifice to cover their shame.

Isa al-Masih supported the "Two or Three Principle." He said that every fact is confirmed by two or three witnesses.[10] This principle is necessary for determining natural and spiritual truth.

An old proverb says, "Many eyes see more than one." Yes, but only if people open their eyes. Many blind eyes see no more than one. Truth is available for those who seek and question and listen.

Children of Ibrahim (Surah 2:40)

Who are the children of Ibrahim? Where did they live when Muhammad was alive? What kind of covenant did Allah have with them? A covenant usually means an agreement, deeper than a contract, where people give themselves to one another. For example, in many

---

[9] Injil, 1Thessalonians 5:21

[10] Injil, Matthew 18:16

cultures a husband and wife make a covenant to love one another for life.

In the first book of the Tawrat, called Genesis (Beginnings), we can read how Allah made a covenant with Ibrahim.[11] He promises to make the children of Ibrahim into a great nation who will enjoy Allah's blessings and take his blessing to all other nations.

Ibrahim fulfilled his part of the covenant when he left his father's house and denounced idolatry.

Did Allah fulfill his part of the covenant? If he did, when and how?

The Qur'an reminds us how Allah delivered the Isra'ilites from slavery in Egypt, parted the Red Sea, destroyed the Pharaoh's army and then led them through the wilderness.

The Ten Commandments (Surah 2:53)

Surah 2:53 says, "And remember We gave Musa the Scripture and the Criterion, there was a chance for you to be guided aright." What is this "criterion"? I suggest it is the *Ten Commandments*.

The Qur'an does not list the Ten Commandments. We find the full list in the Tawrat.[12]

1. Do not take other gods before Allah.
2. Do not worship idols.
3. Do not take the name of Allah in vain.
4. Keep the Sabbath holy.

---

[11] Tawrat, Genesis 12:1-3, "Now the Lord said to Abram, "Go from your country and your kindred and your father's house to the land that I will show you. And I will make of you a great nation, and I will bless you and make your name great, so that you will be a blessing. I will bless those who bless you, and him who dishonors you I will curse, and in you all the families of the earth shall be blessed."

[12] Tawrat, Deuteronomy 5:6-21

5. Honor your father and mother.
6. Do not murder.
7. Do not commit adultery.
8. Do not steal.
9. Do not lie.
10. Do not covet.

Why do we need these Ten Commandments? Imagine a wealthy fabric seller. Everyone knew about his beautiful silk, wool and cotton fabrics. Kings and queens came to buy fabric for royal clothing. But as he grew older, he became deceitful. He displayed fabric under candlelight instead of stepping into the bright sunshine. His dishonesty cost him dearly when a great prince discovered stains on the fabric and ordered the fabric seller arrested and thrown into prison.

The Ten Commandments are like bright sunshine. When anyone steps into the light of the commands, he or she can see the stain and guilt of sin. Like the fabric seller, some people only want to examine themselves in the darkness where their guilt doesn't show up.

Corrupted Scriptures? (Surah 2:59)

"Your book is corrupted! No way am I going to read it." My neighbor hastily handed the Injil back to me. He acted as though it might bite him like a snake. "That belongs in the fire. It's been twisted."

"Hold on, where did you learn that?" I asked.

"The original Tawrat, Zabur and Injil are forever lost. You only have a corrupted book," he insisted.

My Muslim friends, sometimes politely and sometimes not, always tell me I can't trust anything written before the Qur'an. They say the Jews changed the Tawrat and Zabur, so Allah sent the Injil. But then the Christians corrupted the Injil, so Allah had to send the Qur'an. Where did they get this idea?

Surah 2:59 says, "But the transgressors changed the word from that which had been given them; so We sent on the transgressors a plague from heaven, for that they infringed repeatedly."

What does it mean they changed Allah's Word? Could it mean they disobeyed Allah? For example, the Tawrat tells how when the children of Isra'il needed water Allah commanded Musa to speak to a rock so it would give them water. But Musa did not obey Allah's word; he twisted his word by *striking* the rock with his staff in a fit of anger.

Imagine I tell my son, "Please take care of your toys and straighten your room." An hour later I go to his room and find him playing with toys and the room is still a mess. I say, "You twisted my words. Instead of putting the toys away, you are still playing." He changed the outcome of my words. My actual spoken words didn't change. Allah's spoken words don't change.

Muslims, Jews, Christians, Others (Surah 2:62)

This passage sounds peaceful, tolerant and inclusive of all peoples and religions.

> Those who believe and those who follow the Jewish, and the Christians and the Sabians, any who believe in Allah and the Last Day, and work righteousness, shall have their reward with their Lord: on them shall be no fear, nor shall they grieve.

So does this mean the Tawrat, Prophets and Injil are reliable? Without their Scriptures, the Jews and Christians could not have known about Allah and the Last Day. Will people of all sincere religions go to Paradise? If they can reach Paradise by keeping their own Scriptures, what is the point of having the Qur'an follow after the Injil? For that matter, why was the Injil given after the Tawrat and Zabur?

Then there is the question of people who are not Muslims, Jews or Christians. Can someone believe in Allah and the Last Day without having access to the Tawrat, Zabur, Injil or Qur'an? Why does Allah reward people for believing in him and the Last Day? Satan believes in Allah, in the sense that he knows Allah exists. Is it only atheists who are sent to Hell? Could an atheist who does works of righteousness with a sincere heart but doesn't believe in a Creator still go to Paradise? Why does Allah require people to believe he exists, if even atheists can live good lives? Why didn't he simply create everyone with an innate belief in his existence? Perhaps he did. Research around the world has shown that in virtually every human society most people believe in some kind of all-mighty Creator Power. Maybe someone has to work hard to convince himself there is no Allah?

Musa and the Heifer Sacrifice (Surah 2:67-73)

You may remember that the first sacrifice in human history was offered by Allah himself so he could cover Adam and Hawwa's shame with animal skins. After that first sacrifice many more are mentioned. Cain and Abel offered sacrifices. Cain offered vegetables from his garden and Abel offered an animal. Allah was pleased with Abel's offering but not Cain's. Perhaps Cain's heart was selfish and unbelieving. In any case, he murdered Abel in a fit of jealous anger.

What does a sacrifice accomplish? The Qur'an says that sometimes a sacrifice can be used as a sign. This story tells how Allah told Musa to take a piece of the sacrificed animal and strike the body of a dead man. When the sacrifice touched the dead man's body, he came back to life. Signs point to something else. According to the Qur'an, Musa's sacrifice was used as a sign to show that Allah has the power to raise the dead. Is there another sacrifice that comes after Musa which shows Allah's power to raise the dead?

Don't Know the Book (Surah 2:78)

Living in ignorance is like living in a dark cave. Ayat 78 warns, "there are among them illiterates, who know not the Book, but desires, and they do nothing but conjecture."

A cave is also like an echo chamber. In a locked room, the only voice we can hear is our own. There is a saying that some people believe anything passed along, "from ear to ear", like spreading gossip. They have never sought the truth for themselves. If their neighbors spread a rumor that the moon is made of cheese, they gladly believe it. They only believe rumors that pass from ear to ear like a butterfly flits from one leaf to another.

It's not exactly clear what "Book" Ayat 78 means. But the point is that people should not make a judgment about something until they become familiar with it. I'm walking the Qur'an road so I won't be illiterate about what it says. I don't want to just conjecture about the message of the Qur'an. Yet how many people take the time to read the Qur'an? How many actually sit down and read for themselves, not just taking what other people have said?

Confirmation of Earlier Books (Surah 2:97)

Here's a good example of not believing rumors and gossip. Surah 2:97 continues with, "Say: whoever is an enemy to Gabriel - for he brings down to their heart by Allah's will, a confirmation of what went before, and guidance and glad tidings for those who believe."

Rumors say the Tawrat, Zabur and Injil were changed, but this Ayat endorses them. When the Arabs first heard the Qur'an, how could they have known the Qur'an confirmed the Earlier Books unless they had reliable copies? This Ayat assumes that the Jews, Christians and Muslims could sit down together and compare the Holy Books.

> Rumors say that the Tawrat, Prophets and Injil have been changed, but this Ayat endorses them.

Abrogation of Scripture (Surah 2:106)

What happens when a person comes across something that seems like a contradiction in the Qur'an? It is often explained as an abrogation. Surah 2:106 says, "None of Our revelations do We abrogate or cause to be forgotten, but We substitute something better or similar: knowest thou not that Allah hath power over all things?" This is a source of controversy. One Muslims writer says,

> This concept invented originally by these scholars, claims that there are some Ayat in the Qur'an that have been abrogated and invalidated by other Ayat!
>
> The Ayat that is the abrogator they call (Al-Nasekh) while the abrogated Ayat they call (Al-Mansoukh).
>
> Although the concept was originally invented by Muslim scholars as a result of their poor understanding of the Qur'an, yet it has been widely exploited by non-Muslim writers to tarnish the perfection and divinity of the book.[13]

As a Christian, I write as an outsider to this debate. However, just looking at Surah 2:106, it seems to me the Qur'an says there should be no contradictions in Allah's revelation. If Allah says something in one place of the Qur'an, then it should agree with something he says in another place. Allah might reveal something in different words, but the later revelation should only improve on the first revelation, not contradict it.

A different point of view is that Allah can abrogate anything he wills, even if we do not see the reason why. Some people believe this and use the principle of abrogation to explain how a later revelation can

---

[13] "Abrogation, the Biggest Lie Against Qur'an", Submission, http://submission.org/abrogation.html, accessed February, 2018.

seemingly contradict an earlier one.

Praying for Strangers and Enemies (Surah 2:105)

With every sunrise new conflicts erupt in the world of people. Surah 2:105 says, "It is never the wish of those without Faith among the People of the Book, nor of the pagans, that anything good should come down to you from your Lord."

Reading this Ayat made my heart sad! Did the Jews and Christians feel hostility toward the first Muslims? Isa al-Masih taught his disciples to love and pray for everyone, friendly or otherwise.[14] If I follow Isa, then I want the very best for my Muslim friends and neighbors around the world. I don't rejoice when evil occurs. I don't curse them. It should always be my prayer that true life, peace and eternal joy should come abundantly to Hindus, Buddhists, Muslims and all others. If anyone hopes nothing good will come to Muslims, how can they be a true follower of Isa al-Masih?

Stealing People's Faith (Surah 2:109)

History shows that most of the first Arab Muslims practiced idolatry before they converted to Islam. Muhammad preached to idolaters in his hometown of Mecca. After their rejection, he made the *Hijrah* to Medina where he preached with more success among the idolaters in the city. He turned them from idolatry and worshipping many gods to believing in one Creator. This makes the next Ayat puzzling.

> Quite a number of the People of the Book wish they could turn you back to infidelity after ye have believed. From selfish envy, after the Truth hath become manifest unto them: but forgive and overlook, till Allah accomplishes his purpose: for Allah hath power over all things.

---

[14] Injil, Matthew 5:43

If the People of the Book were trying to turn the new Muslims back to infidelity, would that not mean that they wanted them to turn back to idolatry? If they were trying to turn to them back to Judaism or to Christianity, how is that infidelity? We saw earlier in Surah 2:62 that the People of the Book who truly had faith in Allah had hope for a good reward.

Today many people are afraid to talk with a Jew or Christian since they fear the person might try to turn them back to infidelity. But this can't be quite right, since the People of the Book also confess faith in one and only Allah. Jews, Christians and Muslims all reject worshipping many false gods. They all reject idolatry.

Do Jews and Christians Read the Same Book? (Surah 2:113)

What book or books do the Jews and Christians read? Jews and Christians have different ideas about Allah. That should be evident in their different names. Surah 2:113 says,

> The Jews say: "The Christians have naught upon"; and the Christians say: "The Jews have naught upon." Yet they study the book. Like unto their word is what those say who know not; but Allah will judge between them in their quarrel on the Day of Judgment.

Jews and Christians agree on some beliefs and disagree on others. What is the book of the Jews? The Jews read the Tawrat and Prophets (including Zabur). The Tawrat is the first five books of Musa, followed by the books of the history of the leaders of Isra'il. King Davud's book of praise songs is called the Zabur. This is followed by the books of many more prophets like Dhul-Kifl (Ezekiel), Yeshaya (Isaiah) and Daniyal (Daniel). All together the Hebrew Scriptures contain 39 books in one big book.[15]

---

[15] The Tawrat and Prophets are often called the Old Testament or Old Covenant.

Since the time of Isa al-Masih until now his followers accept the 39 sections of the Tawrat and Prophets as Allah's Word.[16] Christians believe that Allah spoke with and inspired the prophets and they wrote down his words. He led them to write about history, laws and commands and prophecies about the future.

The word *Injil* simply means "Good News."[17] There is only one Injil, not two or five or twenty. There has never been more than one Injil or Good News.[18] It could be called *The Best News Ever.* To keep things simple, when I say the Injil, I mean all 27 sections gathered into one big book. The Tawrat, Prophets and Injil all use Surah and Ayat.

Peter, John, Paul and Matthew were all children of Ibrahim who followed Isa al-Masih. They believed that the Tawrat and Prophets all spoke about Isa and accurately predicted his coming. Because Isa fulfilled the ancient prophecies, they accepted him as the true Masih.

In addition, as Allah inspired the disciples of Isa to write the Injil, he led them to use many quotes from the Tawrat and Prophets. Some scholars have estimated that up to 25% of the Injil is either a direct quote or an indirect reference to the previous Holy Books. The Injil weaves into its Ayat the words of the Tawrat and Prophets like a carpet maker weaves together beautiful silk thread.

Nevertheless, not all children of Ibrahim accepted Isa. While many of the first followers of Isa came from the children of Ibrahim, many of them rejected him. Eventually the message of Isa spread across the Mediterranean and into Europe where many idolaters lived. Many

---

The Injil can be called the New Covenant.

[16] For example, the Tawrat is one "Book" made up of five sections or smaller books.

[17] The Greek word is *euaggelion*, (εὐαγγέλιον).

[18] Fake Injils have appeared from time to time, but don't withstand scrutiny.

turned to Isa, destroyed their idols and started gathering together in his name. Compared to the number of these new believers, the number of Hebrew followers of Isa gradually decreased. By the time of Muhammad, there were still some children of Ibrahim living in Arabia and nearby lands who still believed in the Tawrat and Prophets but who rejected Isa al-Masih.

Now we come to the source of the quarrel between the Jews and Christians. The Jews said Isa son of Miriam was not the promised Masih and the Christians claimed that he was the promised Masih. They were not primarily quarreling about the Tawrat and Prophets. Rather, the children of Ibrahim were either not reading the Injil or not accepting it. Unfortunately, it is still the case today that some people are afraid to read *all* the books that speak about Allah: the Tawrat, Prophets, Injil and Qur'an.

Allah Does Not Begat a Son (Surah 2:116-117)

Surah Al Baqarah has many important subjects but perhaps none more than Ayat 116-117.

> They say: "Allah hath begotten a son": Glory be to him - Nay, to Him belongs all that is in the heavens and on earth: everything renders worship to Him. To Him is due the primal origin of the heavens and the earth: when he decreeth a matter, he saith to it: "Be", and it is.

It's no secret that the Injil repeatedly calls Isa al-Masih the "Son of Allah." It also calls him the "Son of Man." The Injil says "Allah so loved the world that he gave his only begotten Son, that whoever believers in him should not perish but have everlasting life."[19] In the time of Muhammad word had gotten out across Africa and the Middle East that the Injil calls Isa the only begotten Son of Allah. It was no

---

[19] Injil, John 3:16

secret back then either.

Though this Ayat does not name Christians—it simply says, "they"—we can assume it probably means Christians. As a follower of Isa I can read 116 and 117 without a strong negative reaction. Why? Because I'm not fully convinced that the Injil and Qur'an are talking about the same thing here.

Consider Surah 5:116.

> And behold! Allah will say: "O Isa the son of Miriam! didst thou say unto men, "Worship me and my mother as gods in derogation of Allah?" He will say: "Glory to Thee! never could I say what I had no right.[20]

Here is a strong condemnation of idolatry. Don't worship any other gods than the one true Allah. A Jew and a Christian would agree and say, "Amen." So what is the problem? Perhaps the confusion comes from the ancient tradition of some Christian peoples burning candles to pictures of Miriam holding baby Isa in her arms. Are these people worshipping Miriam and Isa as gods? Sometimes it almost seems so, even to me.

I have never prayed to a picture or prayed to any saint or to anything other than the one Creator Allah, so I can't speak for all the traditions in the world. However, from my experience even those who burn candles before a painting of Miriam would probably say that they do not consider her a god. She was a human. The Prophets, Injil and Qur'an teach that she was a virgin who became pregnant with Isa by a miracle. She had no husband and Isa had no earthly father.

Yet Christians believe that Isa was the only begotten Son of Allah. This can sound bad, really bad. It can sound like blasphemy. *Shirk*!

---

[20] Surah 5:116 with 4:169 and 5:77-79; also Surah 19:36; 19:91; 112:3

Blasphemy! Allah, having a son!?

Maybe we can find an answer if we think about the word *begotten* in a different way. When was Isa supposedly begotten? Was it in time or in eternity? The Qur'an says that Allah created Isa by saying, "Be". From a human point of view, it's obvious that Isa's physical body came into existence in Miriam's womb at a specific moment of time. But when did the Spirit of Isa come into existence? The Injil teaches something extraordinary. Before even time and space existed, Isa was eternally and spiritually begotten--or coming forth--from the heart of Allah. For this reason he is called the *Kalimatullah* and the *Ruhullah*. The Qur'an uses both of these special titles for Isa. When the Injil says "begotten" it does not mean born separately like a human child is born to his father. It means coming forth in unity with the very substance and person of Allah. It's like Allah poured himself into the human being Isa al-Masih. For this reason Isa is both considered as the Son of Allah and the Son of Man.

Furthermore, the Injil calls Allah the Heavenly Father[21] not because he took a wife and had a son (May it never be! Christians also call such a belief *Shirk*), but because he is the First, the Highest and the one who acts with the ultimate purpose. As an example, people in Turkey still refer to Kemal Mustafa as "Ataturk" because he was the first, highest and founder of Turkey. But he personally never had any physical children.

Here is the big question that keeps coming up again and again as we read the Qur'an. Who is Isa al-Masih?

Following the Desires of Others (Surah 2:120)

---

[21] I generally try to capitalize the word "Heaven" when using it to speak about the place where Allah exists separate from the universe. In some places "heaven" or "heavens" refers to the sky or cosmos. Christians think of Heaven as the place of eternal life with Allah.

Not all human desires are good. Our hearts can often stray from safety like a wayward sheep. The Qur'an gives caution about being misled by wrong desires. Surah 2:120 says,

> Never will the Jews or the Christians be satisfied with thee unless thou follow their form of religion. Say: "The Guidance of Allah - that is the Guidance," Wert thou to follow their desires after the knowledge which hath reached thee, then wouldst thou find neither Protector nor Helper against Allah.

My response, and I believe that of many others, would certainly be, "Yes, we should not follow our desires, we should follow the guidance of Allah." The human heart can often be an unreliable compass. If we are honest we realize it is a fountain of evil flowing with evil thoughts, murders, adulteries, fornications, thefts, false witness and blasphemies.[22] Our only hope is to follow Allah's right guidance in his Word, not our desires.

As we saw in Surah 2:62, the Qur'an says that some Jews and Christians had the possibility of a great reward from Allah. How would they get this reward? By truly following his Word revealed in the Tawrat, Prophets and Injil. Therefore 2:120 cannot mean that Jews and Christians have lost the truth, only that some had abandoned the Word of Allah. Is that what is meant next in Ayat 2:121, "Those to whom we have sent the Book study it as it should be studied: they are the ones that believe therein: those who reject Faith therein - the loss is their own"?

The Ka'aba (Surah 2:127)

Let's turn now to the subject of the Ka'aba. Located in the heart of Mecca, this large cube is 13.1 m (43 ft.) high, with sides measuring 11.03 m (36.2 ft.) by 12.86 m (42.2 ft.). It is covered by black and gold

---

[22] Injil, Matthew 15:19

cloth. A large stone, perhaps a meteorite, is permanently embedded in the eastern corner of the structure. As part of the annual hajj countless pilgrims slowly move in a counterclockwise circle seven times around the Ka'aba. Many attempt to get close enough to touch or kiss the sacred stone.

Surah 2:127 offers a story that connects Ibrahim with the Ka'aba and Mecca. "And remember Ibrahim and Ismael raised the foundations of the House." As a Christian reading the Qur'an, I find this a fascinating narrative from the life of Ibrahim. Searching the Tawrat, Prophets and Injil, I am unable to find any corresponding story. The Tawrat gives a detailed account of the call of Ibrahim in the land of Ur, his wanderings to Haran, sojourn in the Promised Land of Philistine, his journey to Egypt and finally his death in the Promised Land.

I'm curious why the Tawrat makes no mention of Ibrahim visiting Mecca. It could mean that Musa simply left out part of the story when Allah inspired him to write the history of Ibrahim. During his wanderings and travels to Egypt, Ibrahim could have traveled far south into Arabia and visited the city of Mecca. Perhaps he visited a Ka'aba in a different city. But that raises another question. What would motivate Ibrahim to raise a house in Mecca with the help of Ismail?

> Before even time and space existed, Isa was eternally and spiritually begotten--or coming forth--from the heart of Allah. For this reason he is called the *Kalimatullah* and the *Ruhullah*.

Why is this puzzling? First, Allah promised to give Ibrahim land between the Mediterranean Sea and beyond the Jordan River. Mecca is hundreds of miles south of the land Allah promised to Ibrahim and his family. Secondly, how does Ismail fit into the story of Ibrahim's legacy in the Promised Land? Ibrahim's wife Sara became jealous of Hajar her Egyptian handmaid and her son

Ismail, so she insisted Ibrahim send them away from their camp. They went into the wilderness and Allah took care of them. But because Hajar was Sara's handmaid, Ismail was not a son legally equal to Isak. Though Ibrahim and Allah loved Ismail, Isak was the son of the promise, the heir of Ibrahim, born to him and his wife Sara in their old age as a result of a miraculous pregnancy.

Hundreds of years after Ibrahim died Allah instructed Suleiman, son of Davud, to build the holy temple in Kudus. This temple had a special room to keep the Ark of the Covenant containing the Ten Commandments. The Kudus temple stood for hundreds of years and was finally destroyed by the Roman army in the year 70 CE. Before the coming of al-Masih, the temple was called the House of Allah. However, the Injil makes a revolutionary statement. "The God who made the world and everything in it, being Lord of Heaven and earth, does not live in temples made by man."[23] Allah replaced the Kudus temple with living human hearts who gladly received him.

The Faith of Ibrahim, Ismail, Isak, Davud and Isa (Surah 2:135-136)

The Qur'an again calls people to the Faith of the old prophets of Allah.

> They say: "Become Jews or Christians if ye would be guided Say thou: "Nay! (I would rather) the Religion of Ibrahim, the True, and he joined not gods with Allah."

> Say ye: "We believe in Allah, and the revelation given to us, and to Ibrahim, Ismail, Isak, Yakup, and the Tribes, and that given to Musa and Isa, and that given to (all) Prophets from their Lord: we make no difference between one and another of them: and we bow to Allah (in Islam).

Apparently some people approached Muhammad or his followers and

---

[23] Injil, Acts 17:24

urged them to become either Jews or Christians. I assume this means that the Jews wanted the Muslims to become Jews and the Christians wanted them to become Christians, not the other way around. In any case, Muhammad tells the Muslims to adamantly answer, "No!" He says that instead of becoming Jews and Christians, they should stay in the revelation given to the holy people from earlier times.

This creates a serious problem. A true Jew believes in the revelation given to Ibrahim and Musa and so on. A Christian believes in the Tawrat, Prophets and Injil. It's therefore hard to understand how Ayat 135 and 136 are not contradictions. It's as though 135 says, "Don't become a Jew or Christian," and then 136 says, "Believe the same things as Jews *and* believe in Isa al-Masih like the Christians."

Someone might protest, "Wait, Ayat 135 says that Ibrahim did not join other gods with Allah. Maybe the Jews and Christians in Muhammad's time were joining other gods with Allah!" Yet any good Jew would throw up his hands in horror at the suggestion that he believes in more than one Allah. After all, every Jew must recite the *Shema*, "Hear O Isra'il, the Lord your God is one."[24] Likewise, Christians confess the *Shema*. As Isa taught, "The first of all the commandments is, 'Hear, O Isra'il; the Lord our God is one Lord. Love the Lord...'"[25] It cannot be said any more emphatically. Jews and Christians utterly denounce and reject any form of idolatry. Allah is One.

Turning the Qiblah (Surah 2:142)

At some point during the life of Muhammad the direction of regular prayer was changed from facing another city to Mecca.[26] Surah 2:142, "The fools among the people will say: 'What hath turned them from

---

[24] Tawrat, Deuteronomy 6:4

[25] Injil, Mark 12:29

[26] Evidence exists that some people prayed facing the rock city Petra.

the Qiblah to which they were used?' Say: 'To Allah belong both East and West: He guideth whom He will to a Way that is straight.'" Later Ayat 144 says, "Turn then thy face in the direction of the Sacred Mosque."

What happened? It appears that for a period of time Muhammad and the early Muslims did not pray facing Mecca. They faced another sacred location. Most people believe the Muslims faced the city of Kudus, as did the children of Ibrahim living in Arabia. There is no explanation why they prayed toward Kudus, except a hint that perhaps they were trying to persuade the children of Ibrahim to come to Islam. Maybe this was meant to persuade the Jews to accept Muhammad as a new prophet in line with the earlier ones. But the Jews did not convert to Islam and resisted. At some point in the growth of Islam, Muhammad gave new instructions to the Muslims to turn the Qiblah to the mosque in Mecca. Some people thought this was odd, as though Allah was having trouble making up his mind. Muhammad called those people fools for questioning the change of direction to Mecca.

> **Jews and Christians utterly renounce and reject any form of idolatry. Allah is One.**

The changing of the Qiblah reminds me of another story about holy places. Taking a long journey one day, Isa al-Masih stopped for a drink of water at a well in the region of Samaria north of Kudus. While he sat beside the well he met a Samaritan woman who had been married no less than five times! Her shameful life made her an outcast from all good society. Always feeling ashamed, she had come to the well at the time of day she could be all alone. However, Isa did not condemn her but instead offered her "living water" that would cleanse her sin and change her life. She was skeptical and pointed out that her people prayed at their holy mountain in Samaria while the Jews prayed toward Kudus. Isa was not so interested in mountains or temples.

"Woman," Jesus replied, "believe me, a time is coming when you will worship the Father neither on this mountain nor in Jerusalem. You Samaritans worship what you do not know; we worship what we do know, for salvation is from the Jews. Yet a time is coming and has now come when the true worshipers will worship the Father in the Spirit and in truth, for they are the kind of worshipers the Father seeks.[27]

All the earth is Allah's. The heavens are his throne. While it can be good to honor historical places, Allah is more interested in what's going on in the human heart.

Ramadan (Surah 2:185)

Surah 2:185 introduces the month of fasting. Let's read carefully.

Ramadan is the (month) in which was sent down the Qur'an as a guide to mankind, also clear (Signs) for guidance and judgment (between right and wrong). So every one of you who is present (at his home) during that month should spend it in fasting, but if anyone is ill, or on a journey, the prescribed period (should be made up) by days later. Allah intends every facility for you; He does not want to put you to difficulties. (He wants you) to complete the prescribed period, and to glorify Him in that He has guided you; and perchance ye shall be grateful.

Ramadan brings festivity to all my neighbors when they gather for the *Iftar* meal after a hard day of fasting.

"Do Christians fast?" my Muslim neighbor asked. He waited for an answer with wide eyes.

---

[27] Injil, John 4:21-23

"Have you heard of the Greatest Fast?" I asked. "It's the story of a great king who gave up everything to show his power over Satan."

"No, I don't know that story," he answered.

The Injil speaks of the Greatest Fast. For 40-days and nights al-Masih refused all food. The human body can live for only 3 or 4 days without water, so we know that he drank something. But his hunger was intense. At Isa's weakest point, Satan tempted him to turn a stone into bread. Isa answered, "Man does not live by bread alone, but by every word that proceeds from the mouth of Allah."[28] Satan then took him to the pinnacle of the Kudus temple. "Throw yourself down," he said, "the angels will surely catch you." Isa refused. It is wrong to test Allah. For a last time Satan tempted him. "Bow down and worship me," Satan whispered temptingly. "I will give you all the kingdoms of this world." Isa sharply rebuked Satan with Allah's Word. "Then Jesus said to him, 'Be gone, Satan! For it is written, "You shall worship the Lord your God and him only shall you serve."'"[29] Isa won that battle and Satan fled until an opportune time.

Do Christians fast? Yes, but not necessarily at a fixed time. We fast according to our need for prayer. Fasting helps us focus on Allah, not food. It clears our hearts and bodies to seek the Lord more intensely. We also believe that Isa won many battles against Satan and shares his victory with us. Fasting is good, but what Isa did in the wilderness during his great 40-day fast is even better. He proved his perfection.

Fighting in the Way of Allah (Surah 2:190-193)

In later Ayat we will encounter the word Jihad (الجهاد), but here the phrase in Arabic reads, "وَقَاتِلُوا فِي سَبِيلِ اللَّهِ," or "Fight in the way of

---

[28] Injil, Matthew 4:4

[29] Injil, Matthew 4:10

32

Allah." Surah 2:190-193 spells out the nature of this fighting.

> Fight in the cause of Allah those who fight you, but do not transgress limits; for Allah loveth not transgressors. And slay them wherever ye catch them, and turn them out from where they have turned you out; for tumult and oppression are worse than slaughter; but fight them not at the Sacred Mosque, unless they fight you there; but if they fight you, slay them. Such is the reward of those who suppress faith. But if they cease, Allah is Oft-Forgiving, Most Merciful. And fight them on until there is no more tumult or oppression, and there prevail justice and Faith in Allah; but if they cease, let there be no hostility except to those who practise oppression.

A Muslim friend corrected me. "You don't understand."

"What are you talking about?" I asked. I was confused.

"You don't understand Jihad. It means inner struggle. Every Muslim has to fight Jihad in their heart to live in the way of Allah."

We were talking about the Qur'an. "I'm not disagreeing with you that there is an inner jihad. But that's not what Ayat like 2:190 are talking about. This is describing a physical, military battle, not an inner struggle."

He looked carefully at the Qur'an.

I continued, "See, it gives instructions here to kill the enemy combatants after they catch them and drive people out of Islamic territory, even if it means fighting at the Sacred Mosque in Mecca. The purpose of the fighting according to Ayat 193 is to end oppression and cause Islam (Faith in Allah) to prevail."

"I see," he said and quietly handed the Qur'an back to me.

There are many questions about these Ayat. How far does this fighting extend? Arabia? The Middle East? Across the entire world? This passage doesn't clearly say. Is the fight still going on today? Should Muslims engage in military campaigns to advance Islamic justice and faith?

In Ayat 195 we are introduced to the idea that people should not only get involved in the physical struggle but also support it with their personal belongings. "Spend of your substance in the cause of Allah, and make not your own hands contribute to (your) destruction; but do good; for Allah loveth those who do good."

Ayat 216 scolds people who are too lazy or afraid to join the fight in the cause of Allah. "Fighting is prescribed for you, and ye dislike it. But it is possible that ye dislike a thing which is good for you, and that ye love a thing which is bad for you. but Allah knoweth, and ye know not."

Faithful fighting earns a reward. 2:218, "Those who believed and those who suffered exile and fought (and strove and struggled) in the path of Allah, they have the hope of the mercy of Allah: and Allah is Oft-Forgiving, Most Merciful." This Ayat is important because it introduces the word وَجَاهَدُوا (they struggled), a root word for Jihad. Like the earlier Ayat, it seems clear enough from the context of this passage, this is not referring to an inner, personal struggle, but to physical combat. Is this Ayat abrogated by later Ayat? Many more Surah will make us to consider the question of Jihad as we read through the Qur'an.

Hajj (2:196-203)

The Qur'an instructs Muslims about the Hajj in Ayat 196-203. History shows that before Muhammad's birth the people of Mecca faithfully practiced a pilgrimage to the Ka'aba. After Muhammad brought Islam to Mecca, Muslims kept the Hajj but modified it to remove aspects of idolatry. The meteorite remained in the Ka'aba and people continued to come to pray and meditate.

Ayat 193 gives special instructions for Muslims who do not live near Mecca. They can give an offering and keep a fast to substitute for being unable to travel to Mecca.

Looking back to the Tawrat and Injil, we see that the children of Ibrahim made a pilgrimage to Kudus each year for the Feast of the Booths. All Hebrew males and their families made the journey to Kudus to give tithes and offerings and celebrate deliverance from slavery in Egypt.

Isa al-Masih also made the trip to Kudus with his parents when he was age twelve and spent time discussing the Tawrat with temple leaders. His answers amazed them. Upon realizing that Isa was not with them on the way back home to Nazareth, his parents returned to Kudus and found him. Feeling distressed they questioned him and he replied, "Didn't you know I would have to be in my Father's house?"[30]

Cleanliness (2:222)

In Surah 2:222 we think about cleanliness, specifically the relationship between husbands and wives. Bodily cleanliness is very important in Islam. "For Allah loves those who turn to him constantly and he loves those who keep themselves pure and clean."

Looking far back to Musa's time, we discover many laws about personal and social cleanliness. The religious leaders taught rules for washing their hands, what to do with a sick person and how to properly bury their dead.

Cleanliness is healthy, but during the period of Isa al-Masih, religious leaders quickly pounced on anyone for breaking their laws. "Haram!" they shouted, casting fear upon the common people. They not only enforced the laws of the Tawrat, they made up their own laws and traditions. If anyone failed to keep their religious laws, the leaders

---

[30] Injil, Luke 2:49

heaped shame and threats upon them. The religious laws put an unbearable burden of shame and fear upon the people.

Isa saw through the religious leaders' hypocrisy. He said,

> Woe to you, scribes and Pharisees, hypocrites! For you are like whitewashed tombs, which outwardly appear beautiful, but within are full of dead people's bones and all uncleanness. So you also outwardly appear righteous to others, but within you are full of hypocrisy and lawlessness...[31]

Seeing into their hearts, Isa knew the religious leaders appeared to be clean with all their laws, but their hearts strayed far from Allah. What is easier, keeping the body clean from dirt or the heart clean from sin?

Divorce and Marriage (Surah 2:221-241)

Surah 2:221-241 provides detailed rules about divorce and remarriage. For example, Ayat 230 reads, "So if a husband divorces his wife (irrevocably), he cannot, after that, remarry her until after she has married another husband and he has divorced

> What is easier, keeping the body clean from dirt or the heart clean from sin?

her." The Qur'an does not promote divorce, but it makes allowances and protections for divorces to occur. Ayat 233 instructs a Muslim man to provide for the "cost of their food and clothing," meaning that if he divorces a woman after she has his child, he cannot turn her out with no support.

The prophet Malachi gives strong words about divorce.

---

[31] Injil, Matthew 23:27-28

> The Lord, the God of Isra'il, says that he hates divorce, and him who covers his garment with violence, says the Lord of hosts. So guard yourselves in your spirit, and do not be faithless.[32]

Trying to test Isa, the religious leaders asked if Allah allows divorce. Isa replied,

> Have you not read that he who created them from the beginning made them male and female, 5 and said, 'Therefore a man shall leave his father and his mother and hold fast to his wife, and the two shall become one flesh'? 6 So they are no longer two but one flesh. What therefore God has joined together, let not man separate.[33]

No Compulsion in Religion (Surah 2:256)

"Islam is a peaceful religion." My friend smiled widely. I had no reason to think him insincere. He was an honest and peaceful person himself. He added, "The Qur'an says, 'Let there be no compulsion in religion: truth stands out clear from error.'"

"Thank you for sharing that," I responded. Ayat 2:256 is one of the top three Qur'anic passages that Muslims quote to me, so I have heard it hundreds of times.

Believing in Allah is truly a matter of the heart. A simple story illustrates this Ayat. One day a mother told her little son to sit down in his chair and wait for supper. The little boy was naughty and did not want to obey. Again his mother told him to sit down. Again he refused. Finally she told him she would spank him unless he obeyed. At last he sat down, but he said to her, "I may be sitting on the outside,

---

[32] Prophets, Malachi 2:16

[33] Injil, Matthew 19:4-6

but on the inside I'm still standing."

Like this story, sincere spiritual faith cannot be forced. Would anyone change his or her religion for a $100? Would they truly change their religion to avoid paying taxes or to avoid going to jail? Faith that can be bought and sold is phony. True faith refuses to believe a lie regardless of the cost. It is convinced of the truth.

When a Christian becomes a Muslim, has he not decided that Christianity is false and Islam is true? In the same way, a Hindu might become an atheist because she decides that Hinduism is false and atheism is true. People can be convinced by ideas to change their faith, but not threatened or bought with money.

What does "Truth" mean? A true idea corresponds to reality. How do we discover the truth? Ayat 256 says that it should be obvious to tell the truth apart from error. Sometimes it is obvious and sometimes it isn't.

Another story helps us understand this. Airplane pilots depend heavily on the instruments in their cockpits. One of the instruments is an attitude indicator. It shows the pilot his airplane's position relative to the ground below. If the plane gets turned upside down, he might feel like he is still flying normally. His physical senses are lying to him. But the attitude indicator doesn't lie and it shows him that the airplane is really upside down. He must trust his instrumentation. If he doesn't he may die.

Many years ago a pilot was flying near a mountain range when he got confused about his position. The instruments showed that his plane was flying straight into the mountainside, but his body tricked him to think he was flying upwards into the sky. Tragically, he trusted his senses instead of the attitude indicator. His plane

> Seeking the truth means studying, questioning, asking, listening and observing.

crashed into the mountainside instantly killing him.

We can probably all think of times that it is easy to tell the truth apart from error. We know our close friends and we would immediately recognize an imposter. But other times it is hard to know what is true and what is not. We can all agree that there should be no compulsion in religion. Yet how do we find the truth? Isa offered this encouragement. "Ask, and it will be given to you; seek, and you will find; knock, and it will be opened to you."[34]

Remember the pilot who crashed? He could have sought the truth by radioing the control tower and listening to them. He could have sought the truth by checking his instruments. He panicked however and lost his bearings. He trusted his feelings instead of the instruments. Seeking the truth means studying, questioning, asking, listening and observing. That is one reason I am walking through the Qur'an step by step. I want to know the truth.

Resurrection (Surah 2:259)

The Qur'an testifies of Allah's power to resurrect the dead.

> Or the similitude of one who passed by a hamlet, all in ruins to its roofs. He said: oh! how shall Allah bring it to life, after its death? but Allah caused him to die for a hundred years, then raised him up.

The theme of resurrection will come to us many times in the Qur'an. It is also a key theme in the Tawrat, Prophets and Injil. Naturally speaking, resurrection from the dead is a physical impossibility. Once death overtakes a person, the end has come. Yet here is a hint of hope that Allah can resurrect the dead. He can do the impossible. That which is impossible for humans is possible for Allah.

---

[34] Injil, Matthew 7:7

Good Works and Sin (Surah 2:271)

The human condition universally includes weakness and sin. Who doesn't struggle with guilt and shame? Surah 2: 271 says, "If ye disclose (acts of) Charity, even so it is well, but if ye conceal them, and make them reach those (really) in need, that is best for you: it will remove from you some of your (stains of) evil."

This Ayat calls to my attention two things. First, the Ayat warns against doing good deeds for the approval of other people. Isa said something very similar.

> Beware of practicing your righteousness before other people in order to be seen by them, for then you will have no reward from your Father who is in heaven. Thus, when you give to the needy, sound no trumpet before you, as the hypocrites do in the synagogues and in the streets, that they may be praised by others. Truly, I say to you, they have received their reward. But when you give to the needy, do not let your left hand know what your right hand is doing, so that your giving may be in secret. And your Father who sees in secret will reward you.[35]

Second, the Qur'an promises that good works can remove some of the stain of evil. As a Christian I find this particularly interesting. My entire understanding of the message of the Injil, which means Good News, is that Allah has offered a way to remove the stain of our evil. While Surah 2:271 says that charity can remove "some" of the evil, this raises the question, how do we remove the remainder of our evil? If a thief steals his neighbor's farm and then donates one cow to an orphan, is this a fair trade for his sin? What will it take to remove the stain of ALL our evil?

---

[35] Injil, Matthew 6:1-4

Charging Interest on Loans (Surah 2:275)

The Qur'an speaks about money in many passages. The instructions about money contribute to the Islamic Sharia. "Allah hath permitted trade and forbidden usury." Some Muslim writers acknowledge that in the modern world Usury (charging interest) has become the basis of international banking. Money is loaned at interest through credit cards, house loans, car loans, school loans and other loans. People have to pay back far more money than they borrowed. It is a system widely developed and used across the world.

Referring to the Qur'an, many Muslims reject banking with interest. In some Muslim lands other systems have developed so money can be loaned for houses, cars, businesses and other needs, but the repayment plan does not involve interest. For example, the bank can become a part owner in a business it helped start, so that it keeps some of the profits.

The Tawrat, Prophets and Injil have little to say on the question of charging interest. Allah calls greed a sin and he loves generosity.

Spiritual Wages (Surah 2:281)

Does Allah pay spiritual wages? Surah 2: 281 says, "And fear the day when ye shall be brought back to Allah. Then shall every soul be paid what it earned, and none shall be dealt with unjustly." The question of spiritual wages always digs down deep into human nature. Are humans basically good or evil or neither? Why do good people do bad things? Why do bad people do good things? Can humans ever earn enough good spiritual wages to make up for the evil they do? Humans are a complex and contradictory mix of good and bad.

> Like a guitar with broken strings, we have lost the ability to play a truly pure love song.

In the beginning Allah said, "Let us make man in our image, after our likeness. And let them have dominion over the fish of the sea and over the birds of the heavens and over the livestock and over all the earth and over every creeping thing that creeps on the earth."[36] Just as Allah is good and loving, humans can be good and loving. But Allah does not commit evil, so why do humans? The Injil says, "All have sinned and fall short of the glory of God."[37] Like a guitar with broken strings, we have lost the ability to play a truly pure love song.

The result? We earn a spiritual wage: "For the wages of sin is death…"[38] Is there any just way to escape from this death? Our only hope would be for Allah to blot out our sins, as Surah 2:286 says, "Blot out our sins, and grant us forgiveness. Have mercy on us." What does it take for Allah to blot out our sins if our good works are not sufficient?

---

[36] Tawrat, Genesis 1:26

[37] Injil, Romans 3:23

[38] Injil, Romans 6:23

Chapter 3

Surah 3: Al Imran

The Books and the Meanings (Surah 3:7)

We have finished our walk through Surah 2, the longest Surah in the Qur'an. Surah 3 is almost as long. I am a Christian who has studied the Tawrat, Prophets and Injil for many years. I have studied them in many languages, including the original Hebrew, Greek and Aramaic. Since talking to my first Muslim friend in college I have shared thousands of conversations with Muslims.

I have also studied the Qur'an for many years, but I decided this time to write my response as I study it Ayat by Ayat. Unlike Arabic people, I did not have the advantage of learning to read and speak the Arabic language as a child. Still, I am trying to get as close as possible to the intended meaning of the Qur'an.

Surah 3:7 describes two kinds of Ayat in the Qur'an. "He it is who has sent down to thee the book: in it are Ayat basic or fundamental (of established meaning); they are the foundation of the book: others are allegorical." How do we know the difference between the basic and allegorical meanings? Actually the Qur'an itself often tells us when an Ayat is a simile. Ayat 7 continues, "none will grasp the message except men of understanding." Where does spiritual understanding come from? Is it not from Allah?

Hell and Punishment (Surah 3:10)

The Qur'an gives explicit descriptions of Allah's punishment against people who reject the Faith of Islam. Ayat 10 says, "Those who reject Faith, neither their possessions nor their (numerous) progeny will avail them aught against Allah: they are themselves but fuel for the fire."

An Naar or Hellfire is mentioned 145 times in the Qur'an. Other times the Qur'an describes Hell as *Jahannam, Saqar, Sa'eer, Latha* and *Al Haawiyah.*

In the Injil *Gehenna* is the place of torment on the horizon for all who die in their rebellion against Allah. In the Hebrew language, Gehenna referred to a deep valley or gorge just outside of Kudus used as a trash dump. The fires never ceased burning in the valley. It was a place of ultimate loss and destruction.

Why does Allah send people to Hell? Who will go there? What will it really be like? The Tawrat, Prophets, Injil and the Qur'an speak to these questions. The answers must be critically important.

Spiritual Wealth or Material Wealth? (Surah 3:14)

The Qur'an calls people to consider, which is better, spiritual or material wealth?

> Fair in the eyes of men is the love of things they covet: women and sons; heaped up hoards of gold and silver; horses branded (for blood and excellence); and cattle and well tilled land. Such are the possessions of this world's life; but in nearness to Allah is the best of the goals.

This is a question of the heart. Does the heart truly seek to find joy in the pleasures of the world or does it find joy in Allah?

Long ago a very wealthy man owned a fertile estate. His crops produced more than any other, making him ever richer year after year. One lovely evening, as he stood on his terrace and looked across the rolling hills of olive trees, fruit orchards and wheat, he said to himself, "This is amazing, I don't have enough room to store this abundant harvest. Here's what I'll do, I'll tear down my barns and build larger ones for all my crops and wealth. Yes, after all these years I deserve to sit back and enjoy my wealth for many years to come. I'll host parties, rest, eat and drink and enjoy life."

Sadly, after the sun set that evening Allah said to the man, "You fool, tonight your soul is required. Who will enjoy all this wealth you have stored up for yourself?" This is how life is for the person who lays up treasure for himself and is not rich toward Allah.[39]

Davud penned, "the fear of the Lord is clean, enduring forever; the rules of the Lord are true, and righteous altogether. More to be desired are they than gold, even much fine gold; sweeter also than honey and drippings of the honeycomb."[40]

Is gold bad? No, but Allah's words are better. Is wealth wrong? No, but worship is better. Sometimes Allah makes a holy person very wealthy with material things so he or she can share wealth with needy people. But anyone who sets his heart on wealth will be disappointed for all eternity.

Religion and Friendship (Surah 3:28)

The People of the Book are a familiar subject of conversation in the Qur'an. Many times Muhammad expressed the desire for Jews and Christians to come into Islam. He wanted them to accept him in the same category of special messengers as Ibrahim, Musa, and Davud. The Qur'an claims to confirm the books of the old prophets. It holds the Tawrat, Prophets and Injil in high honor. I can find no indication in the Qur'an that these Earlier Books had been corrupted. Perhaps the meanings had sometimes been twisted or misinterpreted, but corrupted? No. The Arabs knew Jews and Christians who remained in their own faith. Was this good or bad? Could a Jew or Christian who sincerely believed and obeyed Allah have a reward? Are Jews and Christians an influence for good or bad upon Muslims? What kind of relationship should a Muslim have with non-Muslim?

---

[39] Injil, Luke 12:17-21

[40] Zabur 19:9-10

Surah 3:28 says, "Let not the Believers take for friends or helpers Unbelievers rather than Believers: if any do that, in nothing will there be help from Allah: except by way of precaution, that ye may guard yourselves." Later in Surah 5 we find a similar Ayat that specifically cautions Muslims to avoid close relationships with Jews and Christians.

Friendship comes in different levels: casual, work, recreation, close and intimate. Surah 3:28 doesn't make a distinction between kinds of friends. Some Muslims take this to mean that their only true and sincere friends can be other Muslims. This makes some sense. An old proverb says, "Birds of a feather flock together." People gravitate toward people with whom they have lots in common.

In the days of Isa al-Masih, children of Ibrahim refused to befriend the Samaritans who they considered *kafirs* from a different religion and nation. They looked down on them. Allah had a different plan for friendships between nations.

One morning long ago a Hebrew trader gathered his products and began a long and dangerous journey down from Jerusalem to Jericho. Around mid-day the path took him through a deep gorge. Suddenly a band of violent thieves jumped upon him. Defenseless against the hardened criminals, he fell to the ground under their sharp blows. They stripped him of his raiment, wounded him, and departed, leaving him half dead.

By chance a Jewish priest soon came down the pathway. But when he saw the steep walls of the gorge, the dark shadows and the flies buzzing around the bloodied man, he passed by on the other side.

And likewise another Jewish religious leader, when he came through the rocky gorge, looked at his fellow countryman, and rushed by on the other side.

Perhaps the half-dead man heard their footsteps quickly shuffling away in the distance. Perhaps he resigned himself to death. But then a

Samaritan came up the pathway, traveling on a long journey. Rounding the corner he immediately spotted the broken body. He rushed over and gently examined the trader's wounds. Showing kindness and sensitivity, he bound up his wounds, poured out oil and wine, and set him on his own beast. Then he did something even more extraordinary. He took the injured man to an inn to recover. On the next day when he departed, he gave his own money to the owner. "Take care of him, and whatever more you spend, I will repay you when I come back.[41]

Think of it. Isa told this story to the children of Ibrahim. They considered themselves righteous and superior to the kafir Samaritans. But the star of this story is the very person they despised.

Isa turned to the crowd and asked, "Which of these three, do you think, proved to be a neighbor to the man who fell among the robbers?" A religious leader answered, "The one who showed him mercy."

Isa answered, "You go, and do likewise." Shouldn't friendship extend across lines of religion, race and nationality?

Resident Evil (Surah 3:30)

Again the Qur'an touches on the deep and universal human dilemma. *Resident evil.* Like the Tawrat, Prophets and Injil, the Qur'an teaches the Day of Judgment is coming. "On the day when every soul will be confronted with all the good it has done, it will wish there were a great distance between it and its evil."

A key word here is *every.* No soul is completely guiltless. Though all souls are created in the image of Allah and capable of doing acts of

---

[41] Injil, Luke 10:30-36

charity, prayers, and believing in Allah, the angels, the prophets and the Day of Judgment, all souls are also corrupted by the evil within. The soul will ache and long for separation from evil. But how? This is the great question of the Holy Books. What is strong enough to take away evil?

The Qur'an suggests an answer to the question in the next Ayat. "If ye do love Allah, follow me: Allah will love you and forgive you your sins; for Allah is Oft-Forgiving, Most Merciful."

I ask myself two questions. Can I love Allah enough for him to forgive me? Second, if my sin deserves the punishment of death, who will Allah punish in my place? If he forgives my sin, does he somehow absorb my spiritual and moral debt himself?

A simple story illustrates this question. One day a great king sent his army into battle. Later that evening his guards discovered that a local soldier had secretly fled the battle. The man had abandoned his post as shield-bearer for the prince. When caught, the villager apologized to the kind king with bitter tears and wailing, begging for forgiveness. The king extended his mercy and forgave the pitiful man. However, at the battlefront earlier that day, the king's own son was struck by an arrow and killed. If the villager had gone to battle as the prince's shield-bearer, he could have saved him. So the king forgave the man, but in a sense he suffered the punishment himself. He lost his own son. No forgiveness comes without someone paying the price.

Isa in the Qur'an (Surah 3:33-59)

Many authors have written thoughtful books about Isa al-Masih in the Qur'an. My Muslim friends are always quick to say, "We love and respect Isa. If we didn't we couldn't be good Muslims." Many Surahs talk about his origin, his birth, his life and even his death. Ayat 33-59 show us a one-of-a kind man. He is the only person ever born without a human father.

Jews, Christians and Muslims have been debating about the identity of Isa al-Masih for 1400 years. Many traditional Jews rejected him as al-Masih. They accused him of doing miracles by the power of demons. They condemned him as a false prophet. They called him a liar and a blasphemer. The religious leaders stirred the crowds against Isa and demanded the Roman government to crucify him. They lobbied the Romans to crucify Isa because Roman law forbade the children of Ibrahim from executing anyone. It's important to remember that Isra'il was under the boot of the mighty Roman Empire for hundreds of years.

Not all children of Ibrahim rejected Isa as al-Masih. His closest followers were ordinary men and women of Ibrahim. His mother Miriam and siblings were Jewish. The Injil says that thousands of Hebrews from Kudus eventually became his strong followers.

> If my sin deserves the punishment of death, who will Allah punish in my place? If he forgives my sin, does he somehow absorb my spiritual and moral debt himself?

We can better understand Surah 3 if we look at five important sections.

1. Miriam's Call
2. Miracle of Virgin Birth
3. Adult Ministry of Isa al-Masih
4. Plot Against Isa al-Masih
5. Adam and Isa al-Masih

Miriam's call is a beautiful story of Allah answering prayer, guiding, providing and protecting. How special is Miriam? Surah 3:42 says, "O Mary Allah hath chosen thee and purified thee chosen thee above the women of all nations." What a great honor! She was chosen above Hawwa, who was the first woman created. She was chosen above

Amaathlah, mother of Ibrahim. She was chosen above Sara, wife of Ibrahim and mother of Isak in her old age. She was chosen above Hajar, mother of Ismail. She was chosen above the mother of King Davud and the women of all nations. Why was Miriam so highly honored? Was she the most righteous woman in history or the closest to Allah?

No. Miriam was a human just like all other children of Adam and Hawwa. Miriam was honored because she was chosen for a *most honorable task*. Surah 3: 45 says,

> "Behold!" the angels said: "O Mary! Allah giveth thee glad tidings of a Word from Him: his name will be Christ Jesus, the son of Mary, held in honour in this world and the Hereafter and of (the company of) those nearest to Allah."

How was Miriam's task of bringing al-Masih into the world the most honorable? The virgin birth was a miracle, but more than that, it was an earthly doorway for the Heavenly Man.

In our physical world we find many unique substances. Earth, water, wind and fire. Out of fire comes fire. Out of earth comes earth. Wind begets wind. Water brings forth water.

Allah is spirit. His essence is spiritual. Does anything issue forth from Allah? Certainly these are deep mysteries. But does Allah wish we remain in the darkness simply because a mystery is deep? Light is hard to explain, but we don't hesitate to use it to find our way at midnight. Surely Allah fully understands and sees himself. He is self-aware and nothing is hidden from Allah. "From Allah, verily nothing is hidden on earth or in the heavens" (Surah 3:5).

Allah is not the universe and the universe is not Allah. Surah 3:2 says, "Allah there is no god but He, the living, the self-subsisting, eternal." I would agree, as would Jews and Christians. Allah has no beginning and no end. Time and space have a beginning and when Allah wills,

50

they will someday end. Earth, water, wind and fire were created by Allah. The Injil says, "For they deliberately overlook this fact, that the heavens existed long ago, and the earth was formed out of water and through water by the word of God."[42] The first words of the Tawrat say, "In the beginning God created the heavens and the earth."[43]

The universe absolutely *does not* issue forth from Allah's substance. It is created by Allah and has a beginning. The universe depends on Allah for its existence, but he doesn't depend on the universe for his.

Surah 3:45 calls Isa the Word of Allah (Kalimatullah). Was Allah's Word created or does he issue from his spiritual nature? This is the question that often brings people to place where roads of belief separate. Some say Kalimatullah means Allah sent Isa al-Masih as a miraculous sign and nothing more. Others suggest that perhaps Isa is called the Kalimatullah because he brought a message from Allah.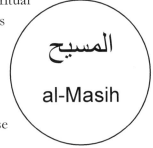

Surah 3:45 isn't the first time that Isa al-Masih is called the Word of Allah. Five hundred years before the Qur'an came to the Arabs, Allah inspired Isa's beloved friend and disciple John to write,

> In the beginning was the Word, and the Word was with God, and the Word was God. [2] He was in the beginning with God. All things were made through him, and without him was not anything made that was made. In him was life, and the life was the light of men. The light shines in the darkness, and the darkness has not overcome it.[44]

---

[42] Injil, 2 Peter 3:5

[43] Tawrat, Genesis 1:1

[44] Injil, John 1:1-5

John originally wrote about Isa using the Greek language. In the original Greek Isa is called the *Logos*. John continues in Ayat 14, "The Word became flesh and dwelt among us."

If you my Muslim friend are still reading this book, we must tread very carefully and wisely. Who is this Word, Logos, Kalima? Here is the deepest of mysteries. From Allah issues forth a personal Word. He is so near to him that he cannot be distinguished from him. Allah's Word in essence is eternal, perfect, loving, the Light (Nur), the Life, and undefeated by darkness.

Later Surah 3:59 compares Isa to Adam. Allah said, "Be" and Isa was miraculously conceived in Miriam's womb. At the beginning of the world Allah said, "Be" and Adam miraculously formed into a man out of dust and took his first breath.

Christians agree that Adam and Isa are very similar. In fact, the Injil calls Isa the Second Adam. But similar does not mean identical. For example, Adam was created out of dust but Isa was born in the same way billions of babies are born. We can't be sure Adam ever had a childhood, but Isa was a normal human baby nourished by Miriam's milk. He played as a little boy and grew into a healthy young man. Adam married Hawwa and they had many children. Isa never married and never fathered children because he was set apart for a most difficult and painful task.

So in what way are Adam and Isa similar? Christians do not believe that the body of Isa was anything other than a normal human body with blood pumping through his veins, just like Adam and every one of his descendants. Isa and Adam were both fully human in their physical substance.

Here is where some may walk different paths. Is there something more to a human than his or her physical body? Since the days of Charles Darwin it has become increasingly popular to believe that all living things, including men and women, slowly evolved from more primitive organisms. Supposedly monkeys and men, spiders and spinach all came from the same ancient great-grandparents. In the modern world, many have concluded that since humans are not essentially different from a jellyfish or an earthworm, we will all completely cease to exist at death and our bodies will turn back into dust, forever forgotten.

Jews, Christians and Muslims believe in Allah, the Last Day and heaven and Hell. We believe that even if the body dies and decomposes, the human spirit continues to live. There is some question about what happens when the body resurrects from the dead, but we believe that there is something more to being human than chemicals. We have real souls that Allah created and these souls live with or without a physical body.

Body and spirit. This is the mystery of Isa who is called both the Son of Man and Son of Allah. While Allah said "Be" and the physical body of Isa came into being in Miriam's womb, where did his spirit come from? Was his soul created like Adam's or was it uncreated? Did Isa arrive on the earth from the essence of Allah as the Kalimatullah?

The great Muslim architect Sinan Mimar is known for his extraordinary mosques. These mosques have stood for hundreds of years, long since he died. A person could say that the esteemed Sinan Mimar lives on through his works. Each and every one of Sinan Mimar's masterpieces started from within his mind and spirit. Before he spoke the words or drew the blueprints, his ability to think and reason and imagine was at work within his essence. The ability to tell stories and plan into the distant future are some of the basic things that make us human.

Sinan Mimar was only a human, though certainly an exceptionally brilliant man. He couldn't actually weave himself (his logos) into his buildings. Today with modern technology scientists have started to experiment with the idea of transferring the human mind into a computer, or more fantastic still, transferring a human mind into a robot or another human body. Idealistic scientists fantasize about bestowing immortality upon humans.

If humans can imagine taking the human mind (*kalima*) and downloading it into a machine or even another human, is it unreasonable to question whether Allah might ever have a loving and noble purpose to do such a thing himself?

"Impossible," my friend said, carefully returning his tea cup to the table. "Why would Allah ever want to do such a thing? He would never need to put himself into a new human body to achieve immortality since Allah is eternal. He would never need to weave himself into a creaturely shape so that he could have more power, since he is already all-powerful. It's disgusting to imagine. I feel dirty just trying. Allah has no needs and Allah is one."

The answer to such a strange and puzzling question comes from the Injil.

> For God so loved the world, that he gave his only [begotten] Son, that whoever believes in him should not perish but have eternal life.[45]

Love can move persons to do strange and bewildering things. Love of country moves people to die in wars on lonely battlefields. Love of wife and children makes fathers willing to suffer under miserable work conditions to provide a warm home and food to eat. Love of man for a woman makes him willing to swim oceans and scale mountains to prove himself.

Love moved Isa. What then did Isa do in his time on the earth? In Surah 3:49 we find Isa giving sight to the blind, healing lepers and raising dead people to life. He does these things by the power of Allah. How else would he do them? Only Allah can do the impossible and Isa is the Word from Allah. Where Allah's Word goes miracles and life follow.

---

[45] Injil, John 3:16

The Qur'an confirms in Ayat 54 that enemies of Allah plotted against Isa. The Injil confirms that these enemies wanted him crucified on a Roman cross. But would they succeed? How could they fight against Allah and win? Surah 3:55, "Lo! God said: "O Jesus! Verily, I shall cause thee to die, and shall exalt thee unto Me, and cleanse thee of [the presence of] those who are bent on denying the truth; and I shall place those who follow thee [far] above those who are bent on denying the truth."[46]

One afternoon my neighbor became very flustered. "Isa did not die!"

Apparently he had never seen Surah 3:55. "I'm really curious," I asked, "Is there any verse in the Qur'an that says Isa did not die?"

He went silent.

I went on. "I know about 4:157, but even that Ayat does not say Allah rescued Isa from death, it says the Jewish people did not kill him."

Love moved Isa.

As mentioned earlier, the Qur'an talks not only about the birth of Isa but his death. It is commonly thought in some places that at the last minute Allah rescued Isa from death on the cross, substituting someone else in his place. But why does it say here that Allah caused Isa to die and then raised him (إِنِّي عِيسَى مُتَوَفِّيكَ وَرَافِعُكَ إِلَيَّ)?

Another friend asked me one time, "Does the Injil say that Isa al-Masih actually died?

"Yes," I answered, "it gives a detailed account of his death in many passages."

First, Isa himself foretold his own death by crucifixion. He told his disciples one evening,

---

[46] Muhammad Asad, *Message of the Qur'an*, 1980.

The Son of man is delivered into the hands of men, and they shall kill him; and after that he is killed, he shall rise the third day.[47]

After the brutal Roman execution, Governor Pilate himself ordered his officers to confirm Isa's death on the cross.

Pilate was surprised to hear that he should have already died. And summoning the centurion, he asked him whether he was already dead. And when he learned from the centurion that he was dead, he granted the corpse to Joseph. And Joseph bought a linen shroud, and taking him down, wrapped him in the linen shroud and laid him in a tomb that had been cut out of the rock. And he rolled a stone against the entrance of the tomb.[48]

John recorded the history of Isa's death, "But when they came to Jesus and saw that he was already dead, they did not break his legs."[49]

A few weeks after the crucifixion and resurrection, Peter and the other disciples addressed a large group of Ibrahim's people and testified,

But you denied the Holy and Righteous One, and asked for a murderer to be granted to you, and you killed the Author of life, whom God raised from the dead. To this we are witnesses.[50]

The Injil says, "For while we were still weak, at the right time Christ

---

[47] Injil, Mark 9:31

[48] Injil, Mark 15:44-46

[49] Injil, John 19:33

[50] Injil, Act 3:14

[al-Masih] died for the ungodly."[51] And, "but God shows his love for us in that while we were still sinners, Christ [al-Masih] died for us."

As with all the Holy Books, to understand Surah 3:55 we have to go back to the original language. Interpretations are useful, but they don't always agree with one another. With help of the internet we can translate the Arabic word مُتَوَفِّيكَ into whatever language we want. I looked in Kazakh, Uzbek, Russian, Turkish and other languages and confirmed that the meaning of the مُتَوَفِّيكَ turns up as "I died," or "I have been made dead."

Allah promised he would not leave Isa in the grave. "For you will not abandon my soul to Sheol, or let your holy one see corruption."[52] When some of Isa's women followers came to anoint his dead body with precious oils, they discovered an empty tomb. An angel appeared to them and said, "Why do you seek the living among the dead?"[53]

The word مُتَوَفِّيكَ in Ayat 55 means to *lift up*. Once in the tomb, wrapped in burial clothes according to ancient customs, motionless as death itself, the corpse of Isa waited three days for another miracle of Allah. The hopeless situation became an opportunity for Allah to demonstrate once for all his power over Satan, sin and death.

Ibrahim was not Jew or Christian

Digging down into the roots of nations we find the man Ibrahim. His name means "Father of Many." From a man who could have no children to the father of millions, Ibrahim was uniquely chosen by Allah to receive a unique promise.

What makes a person Jewish? Simply put, the Jewish people are

---

[51] Injil, Romans 5:6-8

[52] Zabur 16:10

[53] Injil, Luke 24:5

descendants of the tribe of Judah. Judah was a descendent of Ibrahim and his tribe would eventually bring forth the line of kings and al-Masih.

Later in the Injil, the word Jew is used to describe anyone truly trusting in Allah for freedom from sin. It says, "But a Jew is one inwardly, and circumcision is a matter of the heart, by the Spirit, not by the letter. His praise is not from man but from God."[54] This agrees with Isa's other teaching that hypocrisy is like a white-washed tomb which looks good on the outside but is filled with death. Real life starts from within and works outward.

So yes, in one sense Ibrahim was not a Jew because he was the father of the Jews and many people. But in the sense that his heart was made clean by Allah, he represented the deeper meaning of the name.

In a fascinating conversation with the religious leaders, Isa made this statement. "Your father Abraham [Ibrahim] rejoiced that he would see my day. He saw it and was glad."[55]

Ibrahim foresaw the coming of Isa!? Yes, because he was a prophet, specially chosen by Allah. Thousands of years before the arrival of Isa, Ibrahim had Allah's promise that he would someday send al-Masih through his bloodline. Even though Isa had no earthly father, Miriam was of the bloodline of Ibrahim. Ibrahim did not know all the details of Isa's coming, but he rejoiced at the thought of that day.

The Sin of Idolatry (Surah 3:80)

The Qur'an repeatedly warns against idolatry. Surah 3:80 says, "Nor would he instruct you to take angels and prophets for lords and patrons. What would he bid you to unbelief after ye have bowed your

---

[54] Injil, Romans 2:29

[55] Injil, John 8:56

will (to Allah in Islam)?"

The history of the children of Ibrahim recorded in the Tawrat and Prophets shows that over and over they fell away from worshipping the one true Allah and started making and worshipping idols. Sometimes they worshipped idols taken from neighboring countries. Often they worshipped a false god they called Baal. The prophet Ilyas challenged the priests of Baal to a test to prove if Baal was real or if Allah was real. He told them to sacrifice a bull, put it on an altar and pray for Baal to send the fire. The priests of Baal did as he said and prayed. They waited but there was no fire. They wailed and cried and even cut themselves until blood freely flowed so Baal would answer their prayer. But there was no fire.

That evening Ilyas built an altar with twelve stones. He dug a trench around the base of the altar then poured water over the bull until it filled the trench. Ilyas lifted his voice and prayed, "Answer me, O Lord, answer me, that this people may know that you, O Lord, are God, and that you have turned their hearts back."[56] Allah answered his prayer. The fire of Heaven fell upon the sacrifice and burned up everything, including the water in the trench. All doubt was dispelled. The true Allah revealed himself and the people repented of their idolatry.

Led the Wrong Way (Surah 3:100)

Losing faith is a fearful thing. Many people in the world today believe in a Creator. The children of Ibrahim called the Creator by his special name *Yahweh*. The Greeks used the word *Theos*. Arab Masihi still call the Creator *Allah*. Persian speakers use the word *Kuda* to refer to the Creator.

As mentioned, the Qur'an says there is a reward for people who believe

---

[56] Prophets, 1 King 18:37

in one Allah the Creator and Lord of all things.

Is it enough to believe in the One and True Allah in order to reach the reward in Heaven? How important is it to believe in Allah and fear Him? Surah 3:100 says, "O ye who believe if ye listen to a faction among the People of the Book, they would (indeed) render you apostates after ye have believed!"

Who were the people in this faction among the People of the Book? How were they making good Muslims become apostate? Why would they attack their faith in Allah?

It is hard for me to imagine how they were misleading Muslims. As noted, Jews believed in one Creator Allah. Musa wrote in great detail how Allah created the heavens and the earth and then created Adam and Hawwa in his own image. The Jews faithfully said the *Shema*, "Hear O Isra'il, the Lord your Allah is one." Christians too believed in the one and only Allah. They did not believe that Isa was a second god and Miriam was a third god. Just as Muslims, Christians would consider this *shirk*.

Does Surah 3:100 mean that some People of the Book were idolaters, trying to tempt new Muslims fall back into idolatry? We don't know for sure. We do know that the Ten Commandments explicitly forbid idolatry. Isa denounced idolatry when he fasted for 40 days in the wilderness.

We also know that the Qur'an respects some of the People of the Book. Surah 3:110 says, "If only the People of the Book had Faith: it were best for them: among them are some who have Faith." Surah 3:75 agrees that some are good people, "Among the People of the Book are some who, if entrusted with a hoard of gold, will (readily) pay it back."

It may be that some People of the Book really had abandoned the teachings of the Earlier Books. But these people were not faithful to what Allah had shown them. How can any Jew or Christian, then or now, who is faithful to the Tawrat, Prophets or Injil ever urge someone to become an idolater?

Dangerous Enemies? (Surah 3:111)

The Qur'an warns of strict punishment for the People of the Book who rejected faith and broke agreements with Muhammad. But how dangerous were they? Did they present a dire threat? Surah 3:111 indicates that was not so, at least not all the time. "They will do you no harm, barring a trifling annoyance."

This seems to go against popular opinion today. Conspiracy theories abound against certain religious groups. Under Hitler, the German Nazis targeted Jewish, Christian and other minority communities across Europe as a deadly threat to their civilization. Before his empire collapsed, the Russian Czar systematically drove Jewish peasants off his territory. Yet this Ayat calls Jews harmless and only an annoyance not to be feared.

Who is Good? (Surah 3:133-134)

We all admire some great person or another. Boys who love football (soccer) have a favorite team and especially a favorite player. Their star player is the best. He sets the standard for how to play football (soccer). Girls sit mesmerized in front of the video screen watching their star musician. She can dance with the most graceful movements and sing perfectly about love and romance. The young girl tries to copy everything about her star who sets the highest standard of glamor, attractiveness and sexuality.

Surah 3:133-134 speaks of the ultimate reward and the standard for achieving it. It describes the best kind the man or woman, the Muslim ideal.

> Be quick in the race for forgiveness from your Lord, and
> for a Garden whose width is that of the heavens and of

earth, prepared for the righteous--Those who spend, whether in prosperity, or in adversity; who restrain anger, and pardon men; for Allah loves those who do good.

The next world is described as an enormous garden larger than the universe. This would truly be enormous because the universe is now known to be so large that it would take billions of years to travel from one side to the other. The Qur'an says the righteous will reach this garden. Over history humanity has yearned for a way we can be restored to the idyllic world we lost in the Garden of Eden.

Looking around the world today, the question arises. Who? Who is good enough for Paradise? Who is a perfect star? Looking within myself, I discover the desire to do good, but not the power. Looking around, I see wars and

> **Compared to Allah's goodness, I am a star that has tragically fallen to the earth.**

rumors of wars, treachery, unfaithfulness, greed and selfishness. When I lift someone on a pedestal as a star example of goodness, I later see them collapse in failure.

Like a brilliant doctor, the Injil diagnoses the true condition of the human heart.

> For we have already charged that all, both Jews and Greeks, are under sin, as it is written: 'None is righteous, no, not one; no one understands; no one seeks for God'[57]

"Even I, Lord? Do I fall short of your perfect standard?" I look in the mirror and answer, "So it is."

This is the problem. I agree that Allah loves to see generosity, self-discipline and mercy in my life. Yet I must confess I am selfish,

---

[57] Zabur 5:9 and Injil, Rom 3:9-11

recalcitrant and unmerciful. Compared to my neighbor, perhaps I am a star. Compared to Allah's goodness, I am a star that has tragically fallen to the earth.

No More than a Messenger (رَسُولٌ) (Surah 3:144)

Is there any difference between a prophet (*Nabi*, نبي) and a messenger (*Rasul*, رَسُولٌ)? What is a prophet (Nabi) as understood by Jews, Christians and Muslims? How does each group define a messenger (Rasul)? All would agree that the one Creator Allah chooses at times to send messages to the human race using individuals.

In the Tawrat one of the chief jobs of a prophet is to accurately tell about future events. It says,

> And if you say in your heart, 'How may we know the word that the Lord has not spoken?' when a prophet speaks in the name of the Lord, if the word does not come to pass or come true, that is a word that the Lord has not spoken; the prophet has spoken it presumptuously. You need not be afraid of him.[58]

Furthermore, the Tawrat gives a very stern warning about false prophets. What happened if someone claiming to be a prophet came to them and said, "Let us go after other gods,' which you have not known, 'and let us serve them,'"? The warning is clear. "You shall not listen to the words of that prophet or that dreamer of dreams. For the Lord your God is testing you, to know whether you love the Lord your God with all your heart and with all your soul."[59]

Ancient prophets predicted many things. They predicted future wars,

---

[58] Tawrat, Deuteronomy 18:21-22

[59] Tawrat, Deuteronomy 13:2-3

famines, difficult times, the rise and fall of kings and kingdoms, and the life of al-Masih. For example, the prophet Daniyal predicted the rise of Alexander the Great and the Roman Empire.[60] Later he predicted the final war before the Last Day and foretold the resurrection of the dead.

The prophet Micah foretold that Isa al-Masih would be born in the little village of Bethlehem. The prophet Yeshaya foretold that the al-Masih would be captured and taken, "like a lamb that is led to the slaughter, and like a sheep that before its shearers is silent."[61]

Musa prophesied to his people that someday a great prophet would arise. "The Lord your God will raise up for you a prophet like me from among you, from your brothers—it is to him you shall listen—."[62] Over a thousand years later Isa's follower Peter stood before the religious leaders and declared that Musa's prophecy had come true in Isa al-Masih.[63]

The Qur'an says in Surah 3:144, "Muhammad is no more than a Messenger [Rasul]: many were the Messengers that passed away before him. If he died or were slain, will ye then turn back on your heels?" Messengers were mortal. Adam died and so did Musa. The Qur'an asks Muslims if they would "turn back" in the event of Muhammad's death. According to history Muhammad died June 8, 632, going the way of all men and women. His followers buried him in Al-Masjid an-Nabawi, Medina, Saudi Arabia.

The Qur'an claims no divinity or superhuman status for the messengers (rasul) or prophets (nabi). They had a special task, but like

---

[60] Prophet Daniyal 2

[61] Prophets, Yeshaya 53:7

[62] Tawrat, Deuteronomy 18:15

[63] Injil, Acts 3:22

all men, they were born, lived their allotted time and then died and were buried where their bodies remain until the final resurrection. Many messengers lived and died, but only one Masih visited the earth and rose from the dead returning to Heaven.

Battle of Uhud (Surah 3:130-180)

The next passage of Surah 3:130-180 concerns the Battle of Uhud. Tradition teaches that Muhammad was injured in the battle, but the troops rallied. However, not all the Muslims were faithful in battle. Surah 3:167 shows that some of them were hypocrites who refused to fight.

> And the Hypocrites also. These were told: come, fight in the way of Allah, or drive. They said: had we known how to fight, we should certainly have followed you. They were that day nearer to unbelief than to Faith, saying with their lips what was not in their hearts.

Why didn't they fight in the way of Allah? Fear, laziness, unbelief?

Other fighters were offered the hope that even if they were wounded or died, they would be rewarded. Surah 3:172 says, "Of those who answered the call of Allah and the Messenger, even after being wounded, those who do right and refrain from wrong have a great reward." And Surah 3:169, "Think not of those who are slain in Allah's way as dead. Nay, they live, finding their sustenance in the presence of their Lord."

What was the purpose of the Battle of Uhud? Apparently the battle was between non-Muslims and Muslims to see who would establish power in Arabia. Usually victory in physical battle was a sign of Allah's blessing on the Muslim armies. Surah 3:160 says, "If Allah help you, none can overcome you: if he forsakes you, who is there, after that, that can help you? in Allah, then, let Believers put their trust." Therefore, every victory in physical battle was seen as confirmation that they were truly fighting in the way of Allah. Although many Muslims died in the Battle of Uhud, in later battles they had a lengthy string of victories over their enemies across Arabia, North Africa and into Europe.

Putting Away the Sword

The ancient children of Ibrahim fought for land centered in Canaan. Allah promised to give Ibrahim a new land. "Now the Lord said to Abram, 'Go from your country and your kindred and your father's house to the land that I will show you.'"[64] The journey was long and difficult for Ibrahim and his people. Allah led them to Canaan, but a famine drove Yakup's children into Egypt. His son Yusuf was a great leader, but after he died the Pharaohs became cruel and used the children of Ibrahim for slaves. For 400 hundred years they waited in anguish for Allah to send a deliverer. Finally he raised up Musa, who told the Pharaoh, "Allah says, 'Let my people go, that they may hold a feast to me in the wilderness.'"[65] The Pharaoh refused at his own peril. Allah sent 10 plagues on Egypt until the Pharaoh could no longer resist.

The children of Ibrahim escaped through the Red Sea and into the wilderness. But they complained and rebelled, so they could not immediately go into the land promised to Ibrahim.

Where was this land? The Tawrat gives the exact location. "And I will set your border from the Red Sea to the Sea of the Philistines, and from the wilderness to the Euphrates."[66]

After Musa died Yusha led the children of Ibrahim into the Promised Land to conquer and inhabit it. They came against the walled city of

---

[64] Injil, Genesis 12:1

[65] Tawrat, Exodus 5:1

[66] Tawrat, Exodus 23:30-31

Jericho. The army did not attack the walls, instead Allah caused them to collapse. Many battles followed as Allah slowly gave the people the Promised Land. In later generations Allah raised up prophets and judges, like Shammil and Samson. They governed the children of Ibrahim according to the Tawrat. Later still the Isra'ilites asked for a king. Though Allah warned them that a king would make life difficult, they insisted. The first king was Saul, then Davud and then Suleiman. Many kings followed.

During the time prior to Isa al-Masih, the children of Ibrahim fought many wars in the Promised Land. Sometimes Allah instructed them to fight with the sword and at other times Allah miraculously defeated their enemies.

Under King Suleiman Allah's promise was fulfilled so that the children of Ibrahim enjoyed peace and prosperity within the boundaries Allah had given. The battle never went beyond those boundaries.

With the coming of Isa al-Masih, the promise of Allah's blessing extended beyond the physical descendants of Ibrahim. No longer would Allah center his presence only among the physical children of Ibrahim. His greater purpose was to offer forgiveness of sin to people of all races, languages and lands.

Allah's Kingdom is a spiritual kingdom. Isa said, "My kingdom is not of this world. If my kingdom were of this world, my servants would have been fighting, that I might not be delivered over to the Jews. But my kingdom is not from the world."[67] According to the Injil, the Kingdom of Allah does not have political or geographic boundaries. It doesn't have armies and weapons. It doesn't have a Promised Land somewhere on the earth. Isa described it, "...nor will they say, 'Look, here it is!' or 'There!' for behold, the kingdom of God is in the midst

---

[67] Injil, John 18:36

of you.'"[68]

Isa's radical idea shocked the religious leaders. For hundreds of years they could only imagine their Promised Land from the Mediterranean Sea to the desert. Some of them were willing to defend their land with the sword. Some of the radicals wanted to drive out the Romans by any means possible, including terrorist attacks.

In the Injil there is no evidence that Isa was trying to overthrow the Jewish or Roman government. To the contrary. When asked if Jews should pay taxes, he answered, "Whose image is on the coins?" They answered, "Caesar's." He said, "Then give to Caesar what belongs to him and to Allah what belongs to him."[69]

> Nowhere does the Injil instruct Christians to take up physical weapons and fight anyone under the sign of the cross.

On the night of Isa's arrest, his friend Peter tried to violently defend him with a sword, chopping off a man's ear. Isa miraculously reattached the man's ear and then said to Peter, "Put away your sword."[70] That was a point of no return. After Isa's rebuke none of his friends struggled to protect the faith using violence.

What about the Crusades?

A thousand years after Isa al-Masih visited the earth, a system of religious politics developed in Rome called the papacy. The Roman Catholic Pope became the head of an international group. Going beyond the teachings of the Injil their system added human politics and traditions. As Islam began to spread across North Africa, Palestine

---

[68] Injil, Luke 17:21

[69] Injil, Matthew 22:19-21

[70] Injil, John 18:11

and the Middle East, the Europeans became worried. What would happen if Muslim armies under the Caliph based in the Middle East began to threaten the heartland of the Roman Catholics? In addition, the Pope and his officials wanted to keep Kudus open for their pilgrimages. The religious and political powers at the time started brewing like a terrible cyclone that would destroy everything in its path.

I write as a follower of Isa and the Injil, not a follower of the Pope or religious government. Rather than criticizing the motives and behavior of Catholics and Muslims who fought one another between 1095-1291 CE, I want to focus on one simple truth. Nowhere does the Injil instruct Christians to take up physical weapons and fight anyone under the sign of the cross. While individual governments have the right and responsibility to equally protect all their citizens from evil threats, the Kingdom of Allah transcends national boundaries. There is no earthly army of Isa. The Good News of Isa flows from person to person through the word and love.

Second, while the Roman Crusaders considered it very important to protect Kudus as a holy city for their pilgrimages, Isa himself rejected this idea. As we saw earlier, he said that true spiritual worship doesn't depend on any certain city or mountain.

Sadly, the Crusades not only destroyed lives and cities, but they soiled the reputation of Isa among Muslims and brought great shame on the church.

Not all Christians strayed into error. Francis of Assisi traveled to Egypt where he met with the Caliph hoping to have peaceful talks rather than angry encounters on the battle field.

In the 16th century Martin Luther wrote, "If I were a soldier and saw in the battlefield a priest's banner or cross, even if it were the very crucifix, I would run away as though the very devil were chasing me!"[71]

---

[71] Martin Luther, *On War Against the Turk*, 1528.

He considered the Crusades a blasphemy against Allah. He believed that soldiers had the right to refuse to fight in a Crusade because it was a false mixture of spiritual and secular.

To be fair, I should also mention that more recently in the 21st century, Pope John Paul 2 apologized for all violence done in the name of the church. "

> We forgive and we ask forgiveness. We are asking pardon for the divisions among Christians, for the use of violence that some have committed in the service of truth, and for attitudes of mistrust and hostility assumed towards followers of other religions.[72]

---

[72] "Homily of the Holy Father", "Day of Pardon", Sunday, 12 March 2000, https://w2.vatican.va/content/john-paul-ii/en/homilies/2000/documents/hf_jp-ii_hom_20000312_pardon.html, accessed February 2018.

Reading this apology, I can appreciate the Roman Catholic confession of many atrocities. I can also appreciate their desire for forgiveness. Yet I would be happier if there could be an honest confession that Roman Catholic teaching has strayed from the Injil and instead continues to put traditions on equal footing with the Holy Writings.

Chapter 4

Surah 4: Al Nisa

Orphans and Wives (Surah 4:3)

Soldiers aren't the only casualties of war. Fathers and husbands killed on the battlefield leave behind children and wives. Furthermore, the victors in the battle would sometimes take women and children from their captured or slain enemies. The Qur'an gives its solution for taking care of these kinds of people.

> If ye fear that ye shall not be able to deal justly with the orphans, marry women of your choice, two, or three, or four; but if ye fear that ye shall not be able to deal justly. Then only one, or that your right hands possess.

The Qur'anic conditions for polygamy (a marriage with more than two people) are no more than four women and each treated equally and fairly with all the others.

Some questions still exist about whether Muslim men may take concubines. Questions also exist about the possibility of slavery.

Men and women have a built-in attraction to one another. This goes back to the beginning of time. Furthermore, Allah ordained the first marriage in the Garden of Eden and included his "instruction manual."

> Therefore a man shall leave his father and his mother and hold fast to his wife, and they shall become one flesh. And the man and his wife were both naked and were not ashamed.[73]

The truly beautiful thing about the time of first innocence is that Adam

---

[73] Tawrat, Genesis 2:24-25

and Hawwa could gaze intimately at one another and feel absolutely no shame. No shame!

Adam and Hawwa were monogamists. They had many children but the Tawrat never shows Adam taking any other wives or concubines. Some might say this was because the only other women around were his own daughters. But Allah's instructions given to Adam and Hawwa speak of one man and one wife.

Adam and Hawwa set the pattern for subsequent marriages. The prophet Nuh took one wife with him into the ark. Ibrahim loved his wife Sara until they grew old together and died. The pattern began to slowly change with Ibrahim's descendants. Yakup was tricked into taking the wrong woman named Leah as his wife. He was miserable and later married her sister Rachel whom he truly loved and wanted to marry in the first place. His son Yusuf was sold by his brothers as a slave in Egypt. Allah blessed Yusuf and he became one of the top government officials under the Pharaoh. The Tawrat says that Yusuf took one wife from among the Egyptians.

One of the major shifts away from monogamy to polygamy came with King Suleiman. He took seven hundred wives and three hundred concubines from his own people and neighboring countries.[74] Perhaps he enjoyed his lifestyle for fleeting moments, but it cost him dearly because they turned his heart away from the Lord.

After Suleiman many of the Isra'ilite kings took more than one wife. Eventually foreign powers invaded their land and conquered them. By the time Isa was born in Bethlehem, the Romans controlled almost all the lands of the Mediterranean Sea. The period of the great dynasties of the kings was over forever and with it their days of taking many wives.

---

[74] Prophets, 1 Kings 11:3

Wondering what Isa would say about marriage, Jewish leaders approached him with a question. "Is it lawful to divorce one's wife for any cause?"[75] These religious leaders wanted to catch Isa in a trap. If he said it was lawful, they could accuse him of supporting divorce. If he said it wasn't lawful, they would accuse him a contradicting Musa. They weren't interested in knowing the truth, only in bringing shame upon Isa in the eyes of the people.

Isa avoided their trap. He answered,

> Have you not read that he who created them from the beginning made them male and female, and said, 'Therefore a man shall leave his father and his mother and hold fast to his wife, and the two shall become one flesh'? So they are no longer two but one flesh. What therefore God has joined together, let not man separate.[76]

Notice that Isa quoted Allah's first marriage instructions given to Adam and Hawwa. One man marries one woman. Like restarting a malfunctioning computer, Isa reboots the question of marriage. Divorce? Not good. Polygamy? Not in the original design. Two individuals come together to make one new whole. Imagine how beautiful this picture can be. No wonder billions of dollars are spent every year on love songs, romantic movies and books, and (of course) weddings between men and their lovely brides.

Fairness to the Needy (Surah 4:9-10)

The Qur'an shows special attention here to the needs of orphans. Surah 4:9-10 says,

> Let those have the same fear in their minds as they would

---

[75] Injil, Matthew 19:3

[76] Injil, Matthew 10:6-9

have for their own if they had left a helpless family behind: let them fear Allah, and speak words of appropriate. Those who unjustly eat up the property of orphans, eat up a fire into their own bodies: they will soon be enduring a blazing fire.

At the time of the first Muslims in Medina, any number of women and children were left without care because their men had died in battle. What would happen to all these needy women and children? The Qur'an sets up the rules for caring for them. Instead of leaving them to starve, the community (Ummah) is supposed to treat them fairly, allowing them to inherit property from their biological fathers. However, Islam never allows adoption of orphans. Even if a family takes in an orphan, the child is a special guest, but never considered equal to a biological child.

Punishing Sexual Immorality (Surah 4:15-16)

Many passages in the Qur'an seek to establish Sharia law for society. Surah 4:15-16 gives clear instructions for dealing with sexual misconduct.

> If any of your women are guilty of lewdness, take the evidence of four witnesses from amongst you against them; and if they testify, confine them to houses until death do claim them, or Allah ordain for them some way. If two men among you are guilty of lewdness, punish them both. If they repent and amend, leave them alone; for Allah is Oft-Returning, Most Merciful.

In my years of living in Asia, I have learned that many people view Western culture as lewd, sexually permissive and deeply immoral. I can certainly understand why. The Western Sexual Revolution broke all moral restraint by telling individuals to do as they please. Birth control methods and abortion removed the risk of pregnancy. Television, movies and music promote and glorify the basest of acts. Many people in Hollywood celebrate homosexuality, divorce, adultery, sex before marriage, sexual perversion and substance addictions. What is a moral person supposed to think about the West when they see its sexually corrupt culture? My Muslim friends rightfully condemn the loss of sexual mores in a culture that is historically supposed to be "Christian."

As Western clothing, entertainment and behaviors slowly seep into the Muslim world, devout people become more and more distraught. It seems that sexual immorality is a lethal cancer spreading everywhere, afflicting everyone and pulling them farther and farther away from Allah.

In these two Ayat the Qur'an prescribes punishment for sexual immorality, but it doesn't give details about the form of punishment. Turning back to the Tawrat we find the ancient punishment.

> If a man commits adultery with the wife of his neighbor, both the adulterer and the adulteress shall surely be put to death.[77]

In Allah's justice, adultery deserves death. All sexual immorality falls under the category of deeply harmful sin. It can break and destroy families and subsequent generations. Yet so many people find themselves trapped by uncontrollable lusts that they are willing to ruin decades of life for a few moments of fleeting pleasure.

Is there any hope? Human nature has not changed since the days of the Tawrat or the Qur'an. Humans in the 21st century fail miserably.

What does the Injil say? Here we find one of the most extraordinary stories ever recorded. One morning Isa went to the temple to teach the people as was his custom. This particular morning the religious leaders approached Isa again trying to trap him. Into the courtyard, in

---

[77] Tawrat, Leviticus 20:10

full view of everyone, they brought a woman caught in adultery.

We can easily imagine the scene. Bearded old men stood around her, eyes filled with righteous indignation and hostility, ready for the sight of blood. The woman fell on her knees, afraid to lift her face, her terrified eyes staring at the dust. The crowd gathered around in silence, holding their breath to hear what Isa would say.

"She was caught in the very act!" the leaders insisted. "The law of Musa commands we stone her."

Isa sat unmoved. With his finger he began to write something in the dust. The crowd waited. The woman waited.

Oddly, the religious leaders had forgotten someone important. Adultery takes two. But where was the guilty man? Didn't the law of Musa command them to punish the guilty couple? Someone overlooked that fact.

After a few moments Isa looked upon the woman's accusers and said, "He that is without sin among you, let him first cast a stone at her."[78]

Speechless, the religious leaders, from the oldest to the youngest, turned away and left.

"Is anyone left to condemn you?" Isa asked. The women answered that no one was left. Isa said, "Neither do I condemn you, go and sin no more."

In many conversations with Muslim friends, I am often asked, "Isn't Christianity too easy? All you have to do is confess your sins and then go out and sin again."

To the contrary. Isa himself gave the right answer to this adulterer.

---

[78] Injil, John 8:7

"Go and sin no more."

Here we have arrived at one of these critical forks in the road. Does Isa condone sexual immorality? Never! At another time Isa said that even to simply look at another human with lust in the heart is just as sinful as committing adultery. In other words, in the sight of the all-holy Creator, the secret thought is just as sinful as the act. Isa gave a higher standard of purity than anyone in history.

So why did he let the woman go without punishment? Didn't he have the right to stone her, since he was sinless? The prophet Yeshaya explains Allah's radical solution for the punishment of sin.

> But he was pierced for our transgressions; he was crushed for our iniquities; upon him was the chastisement that brought us peace.[79]

It's as though Isa al-Masih, the Lamb of Allah, stepped into the path of the stones that should have crushed the life from the immoral woman. Her wounds became his wounds. Her punishment fell upon him.

Does this path therefore lead to sexual permissiveness? Is this like buying a sexual insurance policy so we can have unlimited sex free of pain and suffering? Is it like telling a child he can play with fire all he wants and never get burned? Is this why the "Christian West" has become so corrupt?

No. Sexual sin still carries consequences in this life. The consequences can be sexual diseases, aborted babies, unloved children, lost trust and ruined reputations. Furthermore, the Injil lovingly warns people that sexual sin—and all sin for that matter—ultimately results in eternal separation from Allah. We need to seek the hope of freedom that

---

[79] Injil, Yeshaya 53:5

Allah wants to give us.

How Husbands Treat Wives (Surah 4:34)

How should marriage be defined? Is it a business partnership, a factory to make children, a hotel for people to live together? Who is in charge of the marriage? Surah 4:34 says,

> Men are the protectors and maintainers of women, because Allah has given the one more than the other, and because they support them from their means. Therefore the righteous women are devoutly obedient, and guard in absence what Allah would have them guard. As to those women on whose part ye fear disloyalty and ill conduct, admonish them refuse to share their beds, beat them; but if they return to obedience, seek not against them means: for Allah is most high, great.

This Ayat takes a strong position the man's role in the home. He is instructed to keep his wife under his authority, even if it sometimes requires him to punish her disobedience by withholding affection or even beating her.

I look at marriages around the world and wonder, does love have anything to do with marriage? We just read Isa's beautiful picture of a loving husband and wife. Allah commands husbands and wives to submit to one another out of the reverence of Isa al-Masih. He calls husbands to the truly chivalrous act of loving self-sacrifice. Moved by unselfish love husbands lay down their lives for their wives. Going beyond merely providing shelter and food, a husband should put his wife's desires before his own.[80]

Incredible!? Impractical!? One time I saw a movie where a husband had saved $20,000 to buy himself a sports boat. He felt he owed it to

---

[80] Injil, Ephesians 5:22-33

himself because he worked hard and faced mortal danger as a fireman. At the same time, his wife's aging father needed a new medical bed for his home. It also cost $20,000. For months her husband selfishly dreamed of his new boat and never once thought about using his savings to buy the new bed. While he put himself first, his wife withered. Eventually she started to flirt with a man at work and fantasized about leaving her selfish husband. When he realized how terrible his marriage had become, he repented. One of the first things he did was take the $20,000 and secretly buy the new bed for his father-in-law. When she learned of her husband's loving sacrifice, the marriage fires reignited in her heart.

Trafficking in Error (Surah 4:44)

At the same time Muhammad lived in Arabia, Hindus and Buddhists lived thousands of kilometers to the east. They had very little if any contact with the Arabs in the 6th century. But many People of the Book (Jews and Christians) lived in the Middle East and North Africa. Caravans had regular contact with them. They lived in villages scattered across the deserts and coastlines. The Qur'an asserts that some were promoting error. Surah 4:44, "Hast thou not turned thy vision to those who were given a portion of the book? They traffic in error, and wish that ye should lose the right path."

Indeed some certainly were! History shows that contrary to the Tawrat, Prophets and Injil, many had strayed into all kinds of strange ideas. For example, some taught that Isa al-Masih had gotten married and had children. Others elevated Miriam to the level of super-saint and started praying to her and other deceased saints.

Errors can only exist when truth exists. There would be no such thing as counterfeit money unless there is real money. There would be no such thing as a mistake in math, like saying 2 plus 2 equals 5, unless there is the true statement that 2 plus 2 equals 4. The existence of errors proves the existence of truth. Even though there have been various errors among Jews and Christians, it doesn't change the reliability of the Tawrat, Prophets and Injil. Otherwise, why would the Qur'an tell the People of the Book that they could trust their own book?

The Unforgiveable Sin (Surah 4:48)

What is the unforgivable sin? Not murder. Not adultery. Not theft. Not violating someone's human rights. According to this Qur'anic Ayat the unforgivable sin is idolatry, or setting up a partner alongside Allah.

> Allah forgiveth not that partners should be set up with him; but he forgiveth anything else, to whom he pleaseth; to set up partners with Allah is to devise a sin most heinous indeed.

Christians and Jews agree that idolatry is a dreadful sin. Who is guilty of this terrible sin?

We know that the Meccans were aware of Allah before Muhammad was born. Muhammad's father's name was Abdullah. The word Allah has been found on documents written hundreds of years before Muhammad arrived.[81] Allah meant "The God." The pagan Arabs believed that Allah was the highest Allah.

Muhammad himself taught that the Ka'aba was built by Ibrahim and Ismail in the very heart of Mecca, the heartland of the Arabs. If so, the Arabs would have known about the Allah from ancient times. Yet they filled the Ka'aba with idols. If they knew about Allah and still practiced idolatry, were they guilty of the unforgivable sin?

Let's think about this. If these Meccans had set up gods alongside

---

[81] "The Arabic & Islamic Inscriptions: Examples Of Arabic Epigraphy", http://www.islamic-awareness.org/History/Islam/Inscriptions/, accessed February 2018.

of worshipping Allah, how could Allah ever forgive them?

Perhaps this Ayat means that Allah will not forgive an idolater if he continues to set up idols after hearing Muhammad's message. But in this case, why does the Qur'an continue calling idolaters to repent if they have already committed the unforgivable sin even after first hearing Muhammad's warning?

What about Christians accused of making Isa a second god alongside of Allah? If some Christians indeed worshipped two, three or more gods, does that mean they could never be forgiven? If so, why repeatedly call them to repentance?

This Ayat makes it very difficult to know who can be forgiven. If anyone has ever set up a false god and elevated something equal to or higher than Allah, it appears they will go straight to Hell no matter how much they try to repent.

Christians agree that there is an unforgiveable sin. Isa describes it. "Therefore I tell you, every sin and blasphemy will be forgiven people, but the blasphemy against the Spirit will not be forgiven."[82] Isa had just cast demons out of a man and the religious leaders accused him of casting out demons by the power of Satan. They refused to see Allah's Spirit doing miracles through Isa. They resisted Allah's Spirit calling them to trust Isa. So Isa is saying that Allah cannot release his grace to people who resist His Spirit. A hard heart denies its need for forgiveness. A humble heart no longer says, "No" to Allah, but "Yes."

Intercessors (Surah 4:64)

Can someone ask forgiveness from Allah on behalf of someone else? In many places the Qur'an warns against intercessors. Yet Surah 4: 64

---

[82] Injil, Matthew 12:31

leaves open the possibility.

> We sent not a Messenger, but to be obeyed, in accordance with the Will of Allah. If they had only, when they were unjust to themselves, come unto thee and asked Allah's forgiveness, and the Messenger had asked forgiveness for them, they would have found Allah indeed Oft-Returning, Most Merciful.

What kind of person can come into the presence of the most Holy Creator Lord of the universe? What kind of person can approach his throne room in Heaven? Could a completely innocent human plead on behalf of someone else? But what if the intercessor carries his own burden of guilt and needs an intercessor? For example, if Adam tried to approach Allah and intercede for his son Cain who killed his brother Abel, what would Allah say? "Adam, do you remember the forbidden fruit? Did you eat it?" Adam could never shamelessly approach the most holy Allah. The shadow of personal shame falls over every human, except one, to the end of time. This is a problem with humans trying to cry out to Allah to forgive other humans.

Unwilling to Fight (Surah 4:74-78)

If a man struggles to quit smoking cigarettes, he may feel suffering and pain as his body craves just one more soothing puff. This man wars against himself.

In the early days of Islam, Muslims fought a different kind of battle. Across the sunbaked sands of Arabia they fought in the way of Allah against those whom they believed were the friends of Satan. Yet some of the first believers preferred not to face physical injury or death. Some of them "feared men as or even more than they feared Allah." The Qur'an upbraids these cowards. It says they can't hide safely in their towers far from the battle because Allah can take their lives even there.

Ayat 95 goes on to say that the believer who fights in the way of Allah is superior to the believer who sits at home. The one who fights gets a special reward. Believers are urged to continue fighting even when the going gets hard. Ayat 104, "And slacken not in following up the enemy: if ye are suffering hardships, they are suffering similar hardships." I can see how these Ayat could be taken as a symbolic struggle for the individual trying to stop smoking cigarettes, but the original intent has to do with physical battle between militaries.

> The shadow of personal shame falls over every human, except one, to the end of time.

Ibrahim the Friend of Allah (Surah 4:125)

What made Ibrahim so special? The Qur'an calls him the "friend of Allah." Allah personally called him and promised him a special gift. The Injil says that "Ibrahim believed God, and it was counted to him as righteousness."[83] Before he did any good works, before he offered his first sacrifice, before he entered the Promised Land, he first trusted Allah. The result was Allah put his own righteousness upon Ibrahim. Why? Because Ibrahim looked far into the future to Allah's promised gift. He saw on the horizon the coming of al-Masih. He trusted al-Masih and rejoiced.

The Jews Didn't Kill Isa (Surah 4:153-161)

This passages portrays the children of Ibrahim getting into lots of trouble. It says they broke the Covenant, rejected the Ayat and killed Allah's messengers. We know from the Earlier Books that the children of Ibrahim sometimes rejected and killed prophets. Isa condemned the religious leaders for wanting to kill him like their ancestors killed

---

[83] Injil, Romans 4:3

ancient prophets.[84]

For Christians, Surah 4:157-158 is one of the most interesting comments in the Qur'an.

> That they said, "We killed Christ Jesus the son of Mary, the Messenger of Allah"- but they killed him not, nor crucified him, but so it was made to appear to them, and those who differ therein are full of doubts, with no knowledge, but only conjecture to follow, for of a surety they killed him not- Nay, Allah raised him up unto Himself; and Allah is Exalted in Power, Wise-

Let's suppose I could read this Ayat for the first time without hearing all the interpretations and opinions. If I could read with the eyes of an innocent child, what would I think?

Stepping back for a moment, I notice the Injil *does not* teach that the children of Ibrahim themselves killed or crucified Isa. Crucifixion by nailing a criminal to a wooden cross was a Roman invention. The Jews executed people by stoning. Davud prophesied that not one of al-Masih's bones would be broken when he was killed.[85] Death by stoning almost certainly would have broken Isa's bones, invalidating the prophecy.

In his first sermon, Peter proclaimed to the children of Ibrahim,

> ...this Jesus, delivered up according to the definite plan and foreknowledge of God, you crucified and killed by the hands of lawless men. God raised him up, loosing the pangs of death, because it was not possible for him to be

---

[84] Injil, Luke 11:47, "Woe to you! For you build the tombs of the prophets whom your fathers killed."

[85] Zabur 34:20, "He keeps all his bones, not one of them is broken."

held by it.[86]

The religious leaders themselves did not kill Isa, though they demanded his death. The idolatrous Romans crucified Isa on the cross. Ultimately Allah delivered Isa to the altar as the sacrificial Lamb of Allah, without spot or stain.

The tricky phrase in the Qur'an could be, "so it was made to appear to them." Does this mean Allah deceived them by putting someone else on the cross in Isa's place? But wouldn't that would make Allah a liar? Who would have taken Isa's place? Judas Iscariot the traitor? Another person? An angel? A Jinn? These are sheer speculations. The Qur'an is silent.

Where the Qur'an is silent the Injil speaks. It says that Isa himself died and his friends buried his corpse for three days. During that time it seemed to the Jewish religious leaders that they had finally gotten rid of him. Isa died and was buried for three days, but he was not permanently destroyed. After great suffering came greater glory. On the third day he rose from the grave. He is alive!

We can look at this in simple order:

1. Jewish leaders wanted to kill Isa
2. People saw Isa die on the cross
3. The Jews thought their scheme worked
4. Allah raised Isa

When we consider Qur'an 3:55 and 4:156-157, we see these points of agreement with the Tawrat, Prophets and Injil concerning Isa's final days on the earth.

1. Jealous Jewish leaders wanted to kill Isa like their ancestral fathers killed earlier messengers

---

[86] Injil, Act 2:23-24

2. Crucifixion was a Roman practice, not Jewish
3. Allah, not humans, is in full control of who lives and dies
4. For three days it appeared their plan succeeded, but Allah raised Isa from the dead
5. Forty days later Isa al-Masih returned to Heaven

I'm not interested in forcing either the Injil or Qur'an to say something not really there. That's not so much a risk with the Injil, because it gives detailed testimony of Isa's crucifixion, burial and resurrection.

> **Where the Qur'an is silent the Injil speaks.**

Like court documents in a murder trial, the Injil shows in disturbing detail what happened. Hateful people spit upon Isa, viciously ripped out chunks of his beard, beat his back with a whip until it looked like shredded meat and then pierced his hands and feet with metal spikes on a rough wooden cross. Weak and in agony, he couldn't straighten his body to breathe. In the end he drowned in his own fluid filling his lungs. To confirm his death, a Roman soldier jabbed a spear into his chest. Water and blood gushed out separately, proving that he was indeed dead. It was finished. The sacrificial Lamb of Allah had died for the sins of the world.

Surah 4:157-158 gives us just a peek through the curtain. It leaves some questions unanswered, but it also calls to mind everything we read in the Injil. In spite of doing our very best, humanity could not destroy Isa. For three somber days it appeared that he was merely another dead prophet. But on the third day death lost. Alive with an indestructible, glorified body, Isa proved his resurrection to his followers and then returned to his original home. Heaven. Until he returns.

Do Not Say Three! (Surah 4:171)

Warning to Christians! Do not say "Three" (ثَلَاثَةٌ). Christians are accused of drifting from true *monotheism* (worshipping the One True

Allah) to *tritheism* (worshipping three gods).

Yet when I read Ayat 171 I say, "Amen." I believe that Isa was a messenger, his human body was born of Miriam, he is Allah's Word (كَلِمَتُهُ, Kalimatullah) and his Spirit eternally flows from Allah (وَرُوحٌ, Ruhullah). Neither I nor any Injil believer thinks that there is more than one Allah. Allah is One.

"Hold on, friend," he said to me. "I've heard you say 'Three' (Trinity) many times."

"Yes, I think I understand you," I said. "But I am *not* talking about three gods."

"So what is the mystery of Three? Isn't it idolatry (shirk)?"

Christians do not believe that Allah had a son in the way a man and wife produce a baby. These are three separate beings. Again, I do not want to impose my thoughts upon the Qur'anic Ayat. Isa is called the Word of Allah.[87] Isa is uniquely proceeding from Allah's Spirit even as he was physically born without a human father.[88] Further, in the Injil we learn one of Isa's special titles is *Emmanuel*, which means "God with us."[89]

Christians agree, do not say three gods! Haram! What do we say instead? We believe that Allah the Creator is fully divine, but not all of Allah's essence. Allah the Word is fully divine, but not all of Allah's essence. Allah the Spirit, is fully Allah, but not all of his essence. Allah the Creator, Word and Spirit exists in seamless relationship as one being in the fullness of his essence. Within himself, the eternal and perfect Allah has lived in love and unity without beginning and without

---

[87] Injil, John 1:1

[88] Injil, Luke 1:35

[89] Injil, Matthew 1:23

end. This is how I understand the concept of Allah's tawhid (unity). Praise to him forevermore.

"No, no, no," my friend insisted, protesting emotionally. "You are trying to say that $1 + 1 + 1 = 1$! Is that Christian math?"

This math example is talking about three separate objects, like an apple, orange and banana. Christians do not believe in three separate gods added together to get one.

Imagine this parable. Step into the sunshine. You see the light, feel the warmth and your skin gets burned from invisible radiation. These three waves equal one wave in perfect unity.

Another Muslim countered, "But why does Surah 4:172 say that al-Masih 'disdaineth not to serve and worship Allah?' Doesn't it mean that he is no more than a creature?" Perhaps it does. If so, I have to respectfully disagree. But the Injil explains how Isa loved and praised Allah while he still acknowledged that he proceeded from Allah himself. How can this be?

Maybe the answer lies in the truth that Allah exalts and magnifies himself. The Zabur says, "O magnify the Lord with me, and let us exalt his name together."[90] Before Allah created angels or humans, before he made the heavens and the earth, Allah existed eternally. Within himself in his Will, Word and Spirit Allah was fully self-aware. He needed nothing. He is eternal and complete love. In his internal Will, Word and Spirit Allah lived within perfect loving unity of oneness.

"That's impossible!" replies my friend, throwing up his hands.

I'm not so sure it's impossible. I can see even in myself that my mind (thoughts) is one with my heart (emotions) yet there are times that they

---

[90] Zabur 34:3

work in two different ways and serve one another. My mind appreciates my emotions and my emotions serve my mind. Sometimes people refer to humans as Mind-Body-Spirit. Does that divide me into three separate humans? Of course not. But it does make me more complicated than a tree for example.

What's the main point here? Christians can't imagine holding tightly to the mercy and grace of Allah without holding tightly to Isa al-Masih. Our love for Allah and Isa are wrapped into one love for One Allah.

Chapter 5

Surah 5: Al Ma'idah

Haram and Halal (Surah 5:1-5)

Strict dietary codes can be found in the Tawrat, Injil and Qur'an. For example, the Tawrat forbids eating pigs. The Qur'an forbids many things too, for example, "dead meat, blood, the flesh of swine, and that on which hath been invoked the name of other than Allah." The Injil instructs new Christians to "abstain from what has been sacrificed to idols, and from blood, and from what has been strangled, and from sexual immorality."[91]

Shortly after Isa returned to Heaven, his friend Peter got a huge surprise. While praying, Peter went into a trance and saw a dramatic vision. A huge cloth descended from Heaven, filled with all kinds of animals. "Take and eat," Allah said.

Peter refused vigorously. "Nothing unclean has ever passed my lips," he said. Three times this happened.

The heavenly voice spoke again clearly, "What God has made clean, do not call common."[92]

The Injil provides a radically basic principle about food and drink. Everything should be done for love of Allah and love for our neighbor.[93]

---

[91] Injil, Acts 21:25

[92] Injil, Acts 11:5-10

[93] Injil, Romans 14:21, "It is good not to eat meat or drink wine or do anything that causes your brother to stumble."

Injil, 1 Corinthians 10:31, "So, whether you eat or drink, or whatever you do, do all to the glory of God."

Love for Allah includes taking caring of our bodies.[94] In 70 CE Roman soldiers utterly destroyed the Temple of Kudus, just as Isa had predicted. No longer would Allah dwell in a temple built by human hands. Our bodies would become his temple. Our bodies are sacred. Out of love for Allah we do not defile or destroy the body. We avoid gluttony, drunkenness, laziness, unhealthy and dangerous substances like tobacco and illegal drugs. Anything harmful to the human temple of Allah is considered sinful.

Love for our neighbor means being sensitive to their needs and feelings. If my neighbor is uncomfortable with wine, out of love for him I will choose not to drink it.

One evening I took my wife to a new Asian restaurant. We couldn't help but notice the people sitting next to us eating a huge plate of steaming meat and vegetables. We hadn't ordered our meal yet and it looked delicious, so I asked the waiter, "What's that?"

"Dog meat," he said, grinning.

Personally I am not comfortable with eating dog, but the Injil does not call it a sin. My Korean Christian friends know I am uncomfortable with dog meat, so out of love they will choose to not eat it in my presence. Love for others guides our decisions.

Washing (Surah 5:6)

Water is one of the greatest gifts of life. High in mountain forests icy waters gush from under the rocks. Pure as dew from the world's dawn, it cleanses, refreshes and heals.

The Tawrat, Prophets, Injil and Qur'an prescribe various washings. Traveling outside the Middle East to India, we can watch a hundred

---

[94] Injil, 1 Corinthians 3:16, "Do you not know that you[a] are God's temple and that God's Spirit dwells in you?"

million Hindus ritually washing in their holy River Ganges hoping to escape sin and a cycle of death and rebirth. Many other religions use ritual washings to seek holiness and escape from evil.

Surah 5:6 instructs Muslims,

> O Ye who believe when ye prepare for prayer, wash your faces, and your hands (and arms) to the elbows; rub your heads (with water); and (wash) your feet to the ankles. If ye are in a state of ceremonial impurity, bath your whole body.

Washing with water has tremendous benefit for physical health. Only in the last 200 years have doctors discovered that washing before surgery prevents infection and death. Before modern medical practices, hospitals were some of the filthiest holes on earth, and some of the most dangerous. Washing saves lives.

Washing can keep people healthy, but what is the spiritual value? Can religious washings separate us from worldly sin and attach us to Allah?

One day the religious leaders approached Isa. They complained, "Your disciples don't wash their hands before eating bread in violation of the traditions of the Fathers."

Isa quickly got to the heart of the matter. "Hear, and understand," he said, "it is not what goes into the mouth that defiles a person, but what comes out of the mouth; this defiles a person."[95]

What's in the human heart? Isa knows best. "For out of the heart come evil thoughts, murder, adultery, sexual immorality, theft, false witness, slander. These are what defile a person. But to eat with unwashed hands does not defile anyone"[96]

---

[95] Injil, Matthew 15:11

[96] Injil, Matthew 15: 19-20

Two points here. First, there is spiritual uncleanness in the heart that no amount of holy water or ritual obedience can scour. Second, this deep sin is far more serious than merely failing to obey a religious ritual.

Is Isa saying that the absence of the religious ritual does not create sin and its presence does not erase sin?

Does the Injil teach a holy washing? Yes, baptism. It is a sign of death, burial and resurrection with Isa. Through baptism a new believer testifies about his loving relationship with Isa. It happens only once at the beginning of a person's new life with al-Masih. Like a wedding or circumcision, holy washing in al-Masih is a moment of great rejoicing and hope.

> Like a wedding or circumcision, holy washing in al-Masih's name is a moment of great rejoicing and hope.

Allah is al-Masih? (Surah 5:17-18)[97]

We circle back here to the key question of al-Masih's identity. What is the relationship between al-Masih and Allah?

> In blasphemy indeed are those that say that Allah is Christ the son of Mary. Say: who then hath the least power against Allah, if his will were to destroy Christ the son of Mary, his mother, and all every one that is on the earth? for to Allah belongeth the dominion of the heavens and the earth, and all that is between. He createth what he pleaseth. For Allah hath power over all things.

May I be perfectly honest as I reflect? First, the Injil teaches that Miriam mother of Isa was absolutely nothing more than a human

---

[97] Consider also Surah 5:69-78. Believers in "al-Masih" do not believe that Allah is one of three in a trinity of gods. This is blasphemy.

being. Of course Allah could have destroyed her body and soul. At the end of her life she died and was buried like everyone else.

Second, the Injil never says precisely, "Allah is al-Masih," as though all of Allah simply took up residence in the human body of Isa al-Masih. What it does say about him is far more strange and wonderful.

Imagine a beautiful diamond. A jeweler cuts it flat, like a mirror with just one smooth side. Imagine another diamond. The jeweler cuts it with three sides to amplify the light. The flat diamond can only turn in one direction at a time. The other diamond faces three directions. While one friend admires one side, another friend can enjoy another side.

This is just a simple parable. But this multifaceted diamond can help us understand Allah who sparkles through his three loving relationships, sometimes called Father, Son and Holy Spirit.

To be more precise, Christians say that Isa is somewhat like one of the sides of the diamond. The diamond is one, but no one side is all of the diamond. Just as I cannot point to one side of the diamond and say, "The diamond is no more than that side," I can't point to Isa and say, "Allah is al-Masih and nothing more."

Could Allah "destroy" (cause to perish, يُهلِكَ) al-Masih? The Injil says that's exactly what happened. It was Allah's plan all along to hand Isa over to death as the sacrificial Lamb of Allah. Neither the Romans nor the Jews could have struck down Isa without Allah's permission and plan. He died, but not permanently.

Sons of Allah (Surah 5:18)

The Qur'an 5:18 says, "the Jews and the Christians say: we are sons of Allah, and his beloved…nay, ye are but men, of the men he created."

Who were these boastful people? They could not have been true People of the Book. The Tawrat, Prophets and Injil teach that all of humanity comes from the earth and returns to it.[98] Did some Jews or Christians think that they were anything more than other humans who were born as "men, of the men he created"? Did they claim parents other than Adam and Hawwa?

It's not possible!

The Injil introduces a different kind of spiritual relationship with Allah. Allah is spirit and has no physical sons. The Injil says, "Yet to all who did receive him, to those who believed in his name, he gave the right to become children of God—children born not of natural descent, nor of human decision or a husband's will, but born of God."[99] Allah can choose to spiritually adopt people like children. Allah is not physical and he does not begat human children. He gives the legal rights of childhood to the ones who receive Isa al-Masih. They are still ordinary humans created in Adam and who will return to the dust. But the relationship with Allah changes from brokenness to wholeness, from the fear of enmity to the security of love. Still, this gives no one any excuse to boast.

Dying for Another's Sin (Surah 5:29)

This Ayat makes me sit up in surprise. Can one human take the punishment for another's sin? How does 5:29 answer? Cain plotted to kill Abel because he was jealous of his sacrifice. Abel refused to fight back, but he told Cain, "For me, I intend to let thee draw on thyself my sin as well as thine, for thou wilt be among the companions

---

[98] Tawrat, Genesis 3:19, "By the sweat of your face you shall eat bread, till you return to the ground, for out of it you were taken; for you are dust, and to dust you shall return."

Injil, Hebrews 9:27, "And just as it is appointed for man to die once, and after that comes judgment."

[99] Injil, John 1:12-13

of the fire, and that is the reward of those who do wrong."

It essentially says, "you will pay for my guilt" (بِإِثْمِي تَبُوءَ). Abel admits his own sinfulness as well as Cain's. They both fell short of Allah's purity, but this passage says only one would face the fire of Hell.

The Injil does not teach that a sinful man can suffer the punishment for another man's sin. If Abel did not go to Hell it wasn't because Cain took the punishment for his sin. However, the Injil does teach that a sinless man can suffer punishment for another's sin. This is called a loving sacrifice. Like a sacrificial lamb that dies under the wrath of Allah, a sinless person can die for another person's sin.

When is Killing Allowed? (Surah 5:32-33)

On September 11, 2001, terrorists hijacked four passenger planes. Two of the planes flew into the World Trade Towers in New York City. Thousands of people died, including innocent children. Al Qaeda claimed they launched the attack in the name of Islam. This angered many Muslims. My friend shook his head vigorously and said, "This is *not* Islam! Muslims never kill innocent people. The Qur'an says if you kill one person it's like killing the whole human race."

I was curious. Many Muslim friends quote from Surah 5:32-33, so I was very interested to read it for myself.

> On that account: We ordained for the Children of Israel that if any one slew a person unless it be for murder or for spreading mischief in the land- it would be as if he slew the whole people: and if any one saved a life, it would be as if he saved the life of the whole people. Then although there came to them Our Messengers with Clear Signs, yet, even after that, many of then continued to commit excesses in the land.
>
> The punishment of those who wage war against Allah and His Messenger, and strive with might and main for

> mischief through the land is: execution, or crucifixion, or
> the cutting off of hands and feet from opposite sides, or
> exile from the land: that is their disgrace in this world, and
> a heavy punishment is theirs in the Hereafter;

Many people know part of Ayat 32 but do not realize that it addresses the Jews, that is, the children of Ibrahim.

This says that killing an innocent person is equal to killing the entire human race. What if the opposite is also true? Can one innocent man's death save everyone?

Suddenly I think of a story from the Injil. As the religious leaders became enraged with jealousy of Isa al-Masih, they made plans to seek his death. During their special meeting, the chief leader unknowingly spoke truly about Isa dying as a sacrifice. "You do not realize that it is better for you that one man die for the people than that the whole nation perish."[100] With the death of al-Masih, all humanity died. With his resurrection all could be saved.

Surah 5:32 recognizes the value of human life, but it says that only innocent people are safe from punishment. What about those who murder or who spread mischief (فَسَادٍ)? What about people who wage war against Allah and the messenger?

The Qur'an in Ayat 33 prescribes their punishment: execution, crucifixion, amputation, or exile. If they repent before they are conquered they may be forgiven.

Without more details, we don't clearly understand the meaning of "spreading mischief" and "waging war against Allah and the messenger." Does it mean only the enemies who fought against Muhammad and his armies in the 7th century? We will learn more in

---

[100] Injil, John 11:50

the next Surahs.

Corruption or Confidence? (Surah 5:47-48)

The Qur'an tells Christians to read the Injil and use it to find the truth. If the Injil had been changed before Muhammad's time, the Qur'an would not tell Christians to read it. If the Injil had been corrupted, the Qur'an would have told the Christians, "Your book is corrupted, so *do not* use it to judge the message of Muhammad." But the Qur'an does not say this. It tells Christians, and in other Ayat it tells the Jews, to use the Earlier Books to find the truth.

This Ayat also teaches that Allah revealed the Injil,

> Let the people of the Injil judge by what Allah hath revealed therein. If any do fail to judge by what Allah hath revealed, they are those who rebel.

This fits with Surah 5:68,

> O People of the Book! ye have no ground to stand upon unless ye stand fast by the Tawrat, the Injil and all the revelation that has come to you from your Lord.

The language could hardly be any stronger. The Tawrat, Prophets and Injil are the foundation which remains unchanged.

Who could have corrupted the Tawrat, Prophets and Injil? Ayat 48 says that the Earlier Books cannot be corrupted because Allah protects them.

> To thee we sent the scripture in truth, confirming the scripture that came before it, and guarding it in safety.

How does Ayat 48 fit with Ayat like 2:59 that speak of people changing Allah's Word? It seems obvious that it isn't speaking about corrupting the actual words but their interpretation. For example, with all due respect, I notice that Sunnis differ from Shia in many interpretations.

98

Both groups use basically the same Qur'an, but come up with different interpretations. For example, among Christians reading the same Injil we can find different interpretations. Did one of them change the message? No, not the written word. But the traditions and interpretations don't always agree.

Friendship with Jews and Christians? (Surah 5:52)

Here is another warning about friendships with non-Muslims.

> O ye who believe take not the Jews and the Christians for your friends and protectors: they are but friends and protectors to each other.

Relations between people of different religions have often been uneasy. As this Ayat says, sometimes Jews and Christians have been friendly to one another. Yet history shows that other times they have not. In 1492 the Alhambra decree by Spanish Catholic monarchs expelled all the Jews from their kingdom. Fleeing for their lives, many moved to Istanbul at the invitation of Sultan Beyazid II. At other times in Europe, the so-called Christian rulers oppressed or persecuted the Jews. During World War 2, the Nazi Germans murdered millions of Jewish men, women and children.

As for children of Ibrahim, they have tended to keep to themselves over the centuries for fear of becoming ceremonially unclean through association with non-Jews. In modern times some influential Jewish people have used their position to mock Christians and Isa al-Masih.

Some people take this Ayat primarily as a warning against Muslim leaders making alliances with non-Muslims. Similarly some view it as a warning to avoid taking a non-Muslim as a patron. In either case, most Muslims agree that it is preferable for Muslims not to live permanently under the authority of a non-Muslim. Others take this Ayat on a personal level and avoid friendship with non-Muslims in order to keep the faith pure.

Sometimes friendships can get people into trouble with hypocrites. We see in the Injil how Jewish leaders criticized Isa for the kind of people he befriended. "And the Pharisees and scribes murmured, saying, 'This man welcomes sinners and eats with them.'"[101] On another occasion we saw Isa offer forgiveness and new life to a prostitute. Moving beyond the social norms, Isa demonstrated giving love to some of those who least deserved it.

The Same Ayat (Surah 5:69)

Nearly word for word in the original Arabic, 5:69 repeats 2:62.[102] Not only is this an interesting repetition, but again it promises non-Muslims freedom from fear and sorrow.

> Those who believe, those who follow the Jewish, and the Sabians and the Christians, any who believe in Allah and the Last Day, and the work righteousness, on them shall be no fear, nor shall they grieve.

The only difference is the word "reward" missing from 5:69. Still, these two Ayat give reassurance to Jews and Christians and other believing people that they have nothing to fear in judgment.

Or do they? Once they heard the message of the Qur'an, wouldn't they become Muslims? But if these Ayat are only talking about pious non-Muslims who have not yet heard of Islam, why doesn't it say so? Once pious non-Muslims hear about Islam, are they then condemned if they don't accept it? The question remains open.

---

[101] Injil, Luke 15:2

[102] Compare: إِنَّ الَّذِينَ آمَنُوا وَالَّذِينَ هَادُوا وَالنَّصَارَىٰ وَالصَّابِئِينَ مَنْ آمَنَ بِاللَّهِ وَالْيَوْمِ الْآخِرِ وَعَمِلَ صَالِحًا فَلَهُمْ أَجْرُهُمْ عِندَ رَبِّهِمْ وَلَا خَوْفٌ عَلَيْهِمْ وَلَا هُمْ يَحْزَنُونَ (Surah 2:62)

نَّ الَّذِينَ آمَنُوا وَالَّذِينَ هَادُوا وَالصَّابِئُونَ وَالنَّصَارَىٰ مَنْ آمَنَ بِاللَّهِ وَالْيَوْمِ الْآخِرِ وَعَمِلَ صَالِحًا فَلَا خَوْفٌ عَلَيْهِمْ وَلَا هُمْ يَحْزَنُونَ (Surah 5:69)

The Bread of Life (Surah 5:68-120)

The remainder of Surah 5 talks mostly about Isa al-Masih. He healed people, raised the dead, reportedly created a living bird out of dirt and provided a miraculous heavenly meal. Surah 5:111 says that his disciples called themselves Muslims.

The heavenly meal is intriguing. On several occasions Isa fed people as an act of love and service. One time he miraculous multiplied five loaves of bread to feed five thousand people. Another time he multiplied seven loaves to feed four thousand. Just before his return to Heaven, he grilled fish on the beach for his disciples.[103] These acts of undeserved and lavish giving demonstrated Allah's love. However, the table from Heaven mentioned in Surah 5:112 fits better with another meal.

Each year after their deliverance from slavery in Egypt, the children of Ibrahim celebrated with the Passover Meal.[104] On the actual night of deliverance from slavery, every household sacrificed a spotless lamb and brushed its blood on the doorposts of their homes. They ate the roasted lamb's meat with bitter herbs and unleavened bread. When the angel saw the blood, he passed over their homes without killing their firstborn. Anyone who didn't have blood on the doorpost suffered Allah's just penalty.

On the night of the Passover holiday, Isa and his disciples prepared the lamb, unleavened bread and drink. Up to that moment everything went according to tradition. But then Isa did something extraordinary. He took the bread and said, "This is my body, broken for you." He

---

[103] Injil, Mark 8:19-20, "'And when I broke the seven loaves for the four thousand, how many basketfuls of pieces did you pick up?' They answered, 'Seven.'" See also John 21:9

[104] Tawrat, Exodus 12

took the cup and said, "This is the new covenant in my blood."[105]

If only we could imagine the look on the disciples' faces! Isa was not offering an animal sacrifice for their ancient holiday. He offered himself! The Lamb of Allah.

---

[105] Injil, Luke 22:19-20, "And he took bread, gave thanks and broke it, and gave it to them, saying, 'This is my body given for you; do this in remembrance of me.' In the same way, after the supper he took the cup, saying, 'This cup is the new covenant in my blood, which is poured out for you.'"

Chapter 6

Surah 6: Al An'am (The Cattle)

Judgment on Unbelief (Surah 6:1-15)

Destruction, judgment and penalty. The Qur'an warns people of the consequences of unbelief. The only escape from the penalty of unbelief is Allah's mercy. It says that Allah alone decides whether he will make a person happy in Paradise or suffer in Hell forever.

The Injil says that this destruction is everlasting.[106] Once a person faces the Final Judgment without having made peace with Allah through al-Masih, they must pass forever into darkness. Once a person is separated from Allah after the judgment, there no longer remains the hope of escape. The Injil does not teach the idea of "Purgatory," a temporary place where people pay for their sins before moving on to Paradise. Allah lovingly offers all people a way of escape in al-Masih before having to face the Day of Judgment.

Is Evidence Important? (Surah 6:19)

Imagine a man who takes his neighbor to court for theft. The judge asks, "Where is the evidence of theft?" The man says, "My gold is gone and I have never trusted my neighbor." The judge responds, "Your feelings of distrust are not evidence of this man's guilt, nor is your missing gold evidence. Perhaps you lost it, perhaps someone else took it, perhaps you never had gold and you are lying to get an innocent

---

[106] Injil, 2 Thessalonians 1:9, "They will be punished with everlasting destruction and shut out from the presence of the Lord and from the glory of his might."

man in trouble."

Law courts and science depend on
evidence. For that matter, everyone
depends on evidence in daily life. No
one would drive over a bridge without
sufficient evidence that it won't
collapse into the sea.

> **We need to get
> this right,
> Christians only
> have one Injil.**

Every message from Allah comes with evidence. Surah 6:19 says
"What things is most weighty in evidence? say: Allah is witness
between me and you; this Qur'an hath been revealed to me by
inspiration."

Looking for evidence is good. Having multiple witnesses is also good.
We need to understand this so we can correct a common mistake.
Many people wrongly think that Christians have several Injils. We
need to get this right, Christians only have one Injil.

Suppose someone wanted to write a book about the great Islamic
scholar Al-Ghazali. From birth to death, the biography tells the impact
of what he thought and did. Suppose several authors write about him
from their own perspectives. Reading several honest accounts of his
life would give us a better picture than reading just one.

Multiple witnesses are always better than one. That's one reason why
Allah inspired several witnesses to write about Isa al-Masih. We can
read the testimonies of Matthew, Mark, Luke, John and Paul. They
wrote in harmony as witnesses who either spent time with Isa or spent
time talking to Isa's closest friends. For example, John wrote, "We
proclaim to you what we have seen and heard."[107] Luke wrote, "Many
have undertaken to draw up an account of the things that have been
fulfilled among us, just as they were handed down to us by those who

---

[107] Injil, 1 John 1:3

from the first were eyewitnesses and servants of the word."[108]

We have seen that the Qur'an confirms Isa's many miracles and Surah 3:55 says that Allah caused him to die and rise again. Is there more evidence that Isa was raised from the dead? Paul of Tarsus wrote that Isa was killed, raised from the dead and then appeared to his closest friends and five hundred followers at one time.[109]

Hundreds of people saw Isa arrested by the Romans. They saw him carry his cross through the streets of Kudus. They saw him nailed to the Roman cross on a hill outside the city walls. They saw the Roman soldier stab his side with a spear. They saw his lifeless body removed from the cross and wrapped in burial cloths. They saw his tomb. They saw him buried.

On the third day, against all expectations, some women followers and then some of the men witnessed Isa alive and well. He spent forty days on the earth and during that time appeared to more than five hundred people!

One evidence for Isa's life is hundreds of reliable witnesses. These people had no reason to lie. They knew that following Isa might land them in prison or executed. All but one of the original twelve disciples were eventually executed for following Isa. They saw Isa living again after his brutal execution, they touched the nail-prints in his hands, they ate grilled fish with him on the seashore. How could there be any doubt?

Evidence is very important.

"Where do you think the Qur'an came from? From Allah?" I often get this question. Humans are curious creatures. Like a close friend

---

[108] Injil, Luke 1:1-2

[109] Injil, 1 Corinthians 15:3-7

digging through our kitchen cabinets people want to know, "Where did you get this, and this, and this?"

Ordinary things have ordinary origins. Tomatoes first grew in America and coffee came from Africa. The Tawrat, Prophets, Injil and Qur'an claim an extraordinary origin. They claim to be a revelation from Allah.

Here we come to a fork in the road. In the Tawrat, Prophets and Injil, we discover Allah speaking directly to human beings called prophets. They proclaimed his message. For example, Allah sent the Pharaoh a message through Musa, "Then the Lord said to Musa, 'Go to Pharaoh and say to him, "This is what the Lord says: Let my people go, so that they may worship me."'"[110] Rather than speaking through an angel to the prophet Musa, Allah spoke directly to Musa, as though you and I might speak with our best friends.

The Injil says that Allah shifted from speaking through prophets to direct conversation with all humanity through al-Masih. "In the past God spoke to our ancestors through the prophets at many times and in various ways, but in these last days he has spoken to us by his Son [al-Masih], whom he appointed heir of all things, and through whom also he made the universe."[111] Al-Masih Isa didn't simply speak Allah's Word (*Kalima*), he was himself Kalimatullah. Brought forth to the earth from Allah in Heaven, everything Isa said and did was Allah's message of Good News.

Surah 16:102 offers its explanation of the source of the Qur'an, "the Holy spirit has brought the revelation from thy Lord in truth." Muslims think the "holy spirit" is a reference to the angel Jibril. For example, they believe the angel Jibril was the Holy Spirit who gave the

---

[110] Tawrat, Exodus 8:1

[111] Injil, Hebrews 1:1-2

revelation to Isa al-Masih.

At this juncture, I linger and wonder. Two unique and cherished paths stretch out before us.[112] In faith Christians follow the path that finds its fulfillment in Allah's Kalimatullah, Isa al-Masih. The Islamic path follows the message believed to have come through the angel Jibril. Where will these divergent paths lead? Gazing down the pathway of Isa Kalimatullah we see One Word, full of grace and truth. Along the other path we see the angel Jibril bringing a message of severe warning against Shirk. We all agree that Shirk is catastrophic. What do we think about the Kalimatullah full of grace and truth?

Death on the Sea? (Surah 6:63-64)

Sailors can have unique knowledge of gut-wrenching terror caused by giant waves and violent winds. Storms cause the ship's skeleton to groan from the pain of impending death. Surah 63 asks, "who is it that delivereth you from the dark recesses of land sea, when ye call upon him in humility and silent terror?"

This dreadful picture takes me to a fragile first-century sailboat on the Sea of Galilee. A boatload of fishermen friends of Isa pushed off from shore. With fear and respect Isa and his twelve friends surveyed the sea like a man eyes a wild beast. This night great fear would pierce them like nails.

It started with brisk winds and choppy waves. The Sea of Galilee is hundreds of meters below ocean level. Black as night, huge clouds crushed the deep valley with immense weight. Waters erupted. The

---

[112] I understand that many Jews reject Isa as "al-Masih". But I'm thinking of the fact that the first Christians found Isa al-Masih revealed in the Tawrat, Prophets (including Zabur). Modern Jews today are also discovering Isa al-Masih in the Tawrat and Prophets. They are called Masihi Jews. Followers of Isa al-Masih regard the Tawrat, Prophets and Injil as a complete book called the Holy Book (Bible).

little sailboat quickly filled. Just a dot on the big sea, they listed helplessly under the merciless waves. Grown men screamed and cried out in terror. "Help us!"

Oddly, Isa lay sleeping on a pillow in the back of the boat, unbothered by the howling storm. Instead, the cry of his friends roused him.

Isa stood up. He told the wind to stop. He spoke to the sea, "Peace, be still."

In an instant everything calmed down. The disciples looked at the waves. They looked at the water in their boat. They looked at Isa. They looked at one another in awe and whispered, "Who is this? Even the wind and the waves obey him!?"[113]

Isa averted death on the sea. This is a central purpose of Isa's life. He averts death. He delivers people from destruction and ruin. When Isa sails by, he leaves peace in his wake.

Kill Not Your Children (Surah 6:151)

Though repulsive to our minds, the practice of child sacrifice or killing children has been found in many societies. Before Muhammad came the Arabs had a practice of burying their female children in the sand. Other societies have preferred male children over females and left their baby girls outside to die. In ancient times, some of the Middle Eastern peoples including the Jews offered their own children as sacrifices to idols.

Science in the 21st century has brought a new kind of murder of children. In hospitals around the world medical personnel—who should save lives--regularly extract unborn children from their mothers' wombs. Various abortion techniques kill the unborn human being and then dispose of the broken little body.

---

[113] Injil, Mark 4:41

The Qur'an says, "be good to your parents; kill not your children on a plea of want." This Ayat echoes the Ten Commandments. From the first family of Adam and Hawwa to the present, the relationships that develop between parents and children should enhance and protect life. The 6th century Arabs responded to the prohibition to killing their children and ended the practice.

Why Was the Qur'an Given? (Surah 6:155-156)

"Allah had to send the Qur'an," my friend said.

"What was the reason?" I asked

"Because people irreparably corrupted the Tawrat, Prophets and Injil. Everything was lost."

The argument makes sense, but it isn't found in the Qur'an.

> And this is a book which we have revealed as a blessing: so follow it and be righteous, that ye may receive mercy: Lest ye should say: the book was sent down to two peoples before us, and for our part, we remained unacquainted with all that they learned by assiduous study;

This passage does not say that the Earlier Books were corrupted. On the contrary, it say the Arabs at that time were unacquainted with the Earlier Books but the Jews and Christians studied them carefully. If the Earlier Books had been corrupted, the Arabs could have a legitimate excuse for their spiritual ignorance and say, "we were deceived by the Earlier Books." Also, why did the Jews and Christians study their books if they were corrupted? They devoted themselves to careful study and became knowledgeable in the things of Allah. This proves again that Jews and Christians highly valued and trusted their books.

It appears that the Arabs either did not have access to the Tawrat, Prophets and Injil or perhaps they didn't know how to read those books. The Qur'an simply says that it was given to the Arabs so they would have their own book, just like the Jews and Christians had theirs.

Chapter 7

Surah 7: Al A'raf (The Heights)

The Scale of Good and Bad (Surah 7:8-9)

What will happen on Judgment Day?

> The balance that day will be true: those whose scale Will be heavy, will prosper: Those whose scale will be light, will be light, will find their souls In perdition for that they wrongfully treated Our signs.

Many years ago in a large Asian city a Muslim and Christian met to discuss the Judgment Day. The Muslim friend said, "Allah will take all my good and put it on one side of the scale then take my sins and put them on the other scale. The heaviest side will determine if I go to Paradise or Jahannam, Inshallah."

His Christian friend took a small scale and put it on the table between them. "Something like this, I think? But there's a problem." He filled one side with rocks. "Our sins are a heavy offense to a holy God." He placed some feathers on the other side. "Compared to Allah's standards, our goodness is light as a feather." The scale didn't move.

The Muslim friend studied the scale for a moment. "Then what hope do we have?"

The Christian friend took a large brick out of his bag and plunked it on top of the feathers. The scale suddenly fell to the table. "Can you see? This brick represents Isa al-Masih's perfect righteousness, his light (*Nur*). He lovingly shares his righteousness with his trusting friends."

"Think of this," he continued. "The prophet Yeshaya said, 'All of us have become like one who is unclean, and all our righteous acts are like filthy rags; we all shrivel up like a leaf, and like the wind our sins sweep us away'"[114]

"That doesn't sound correct. How can Allah share his righteousness with us?"

Yet even the Qur'an 7:26 speaks of Allah sharing his righteousness.

> O ye Children of Adam! we shall have bestowed raiment upon you to cover your shame, as well as to be an adornment to you. But the raiment of righteousness- that is the best. Such are among the Signs of Allah, that they may receive admonition!

The Injil says that the pure may approach Allah because they have "washed their robes, and made them white in the blood of the Lamb." Allah's love pardons our sin. Allah's grace shares his righteousness with us.

The Eye of the Needle (Surah 7:40)

Escape for sinners is no more possible than it is for a camel to pass through the eye of the needle.

> To those who reject Our Signs and treat them with arrogance, no opening will there be of the gates of heaven, nor will they enter the Garden, until the camel can pass through the eye of the needle: such is Our reward for those

---

[114] Prophets, Yeshaya 64:6

in sin.

One day a rich man came to Isa asking about eternal life. He told the young man to sell everything and follow him. "No," said the man, Isa was asking for all his love, not just a part.

Later Isa told his disciples, "Again I tell you, it is easier for a camel to go through the eye of a needle than for someone who is rich to enter the kingdom of God"[115] The stunned disciples asked, "who then can be saved?" If all rich people and all who want to be rich are beyond salvation, what hope is there?

Isa shifted their attention upwards. "With man this is impossible, but with God all things are possible."[116]

What is Allah's attitude about judging sinners? He says, "'As surely as I live,' declares the Sovereign Lord, 'I take no pleasure in the death of the wicked, but rather that they turn from their ways and live.'"[117]

Isa says that Allah did not send him into the world to condemn it, but that through him the world may be saved.[118]

Allah Visits Earth (Surah 7:143)

Surah 7:143 lists many prophets. Nuh went to his people. Hud spoke to the Aad. Salih went to Thamud. Lut went to his people, who came under judgment for sexual perversion and sin. Shu'aib went to the Madyan people. In each case the Qur'an says that a prophet spoke Allah's warnings but many people didn't believe and then suffered destruction. There is a certain order: rebellious people, messenger,

---

[115] Injil, Matthew 19:24

[116] Injil, Matthew 19:26

[117] Prophets, Ezekiel 33:11

[118] Injil, John 3:17

rejection of the messenger, Allah's punishment.

Ayat 103 introduces Musa. He went to the Pharaoh with a command from Allah to release the Hebrew slaves. The Egyptians resisted Musa even after a series of terrible judgments that included water turning to blood, fire and hail from the sky and an invasion of frogs into their cities. Suddenly in Ayat 143 we discover an earth-shaking encounter between Allah and this world.

What is so surprising? One of the key differences in the Muslim and Christian understandings of Allah is their view of Allah's relationship with time and space. Many friends have asked, "If Allah was in Isa al-Masih on the cross, who was in Heaven? If Allah vacated Heaven, who would continue to reign over all things? Would Allah step away from his throne and let everything collapse into chaos?"

I've already offered a picture of Perfect Love folded in upon himself in three ways. One fold of Perfect Love was Isa Masih living in time and space. At precisely the same time Perfect Love reigned on the throne of Heaven. Allah is One.

Is this absurd? Allah on earth and Allah in Heaven? Here is the Qur'an's big surprise. Surah 7:143,

> When Musa came to the place appointed by us, and his Lord addressed him, he said: O my Lord show to me, that I may look upon thee. Allah said. By no means canst thou see me; but look upon the mount; if it abide in its place, then shalt thou see me. When his Lord manifested his glory on the mount, He made it as dust, and Musa fell down in a swoon. When he recovered his senses he said: Glory be to thee to thee I turn in repentance, and I am the first to believe.

This story also appears in the Tawrat. Musa prayed, "Show me you glory."[119] Allah replied,

> He said, "you cannot see my face, for no one may see me
> and live." Then the Lord said, "There is a place near me
> where you may stand on a rock. When my glory passes by,
> I will put you in a cleft in the rock and cover you with my
> hand until I have passed by. Then I will remove my hand
> and you will see my back; but my face must not be seen."[120]

The Qur'an and the Tawrat confirm that Allah can manifest himself in time and space. When Allah was on the mountain with Musa, who was in Heaven? Was the almighty throne of Heaven vacant? May it never be!

It is easy to say all things are possible with Allah. Most people believe all things are possible that are reasonable. Could Allah make an object so heavy that he couldn't pick it up? Can Allah make a square circle? These are logical impossibilities. Is it a logically impossible for Allah to be present both on the mountain with Musa and on his throne in Heaven?

Part of the answer to this problem can be found in the first Surah of the Tawrat. "God saw all that he had made, and it was very good."[121] The physical world was good, because Allah made it. The mountains, flowers, trees, animals and humans were good in their physical form. When Adam and Hawwa sinned against God, it made their spiritual life plummet into a state of corruption. But it didn't change the goodness of the stars and sky and rivers and deserts. Allah could enter the physical world as he wished because in no way did it spoil his own

---

[119] Tawrat, Exodus 33:18

[120] Tawrat, Exodus 33:20-23

[121] Tawrat, Genesis 1:31

goodness and honor.

But how could Allah be in two different places at once? Allah is not limited by space. In some sense he fills everything. Davud asked, "Where can I go from your Spirit? Where can I flee from your presence? If I go up to the heavens, you are there; if I make my bed in the depths, you are there."[122]

But there could be a deeper answer. The Word of Allah comes forth from Allah as an expression of his love. When we say "Word", we mean much more than spoken words in a conversation. The Word is the very essence of Allah's mind. Therefore it is possible that Allah in his authority remains on his throne while Allah in his loving Word makes special visitations to the earth. Allah visited Musa on the mountain and years earlier he visited Musa in a burning bush that was not consumed.[123] He visited Ibrahim with three "men" before he destroyed Sodom and Gomorrah.[124] The final such visitation according to the Injil occurred in al-Masih. This was the pinnacle of Allah entering time and space. He had done it before, but only briefly as though passing by on a journey. In al-Masih Allah walked among his people, full of grace and truth.[125]

Judged by the Ten Commandments (Surah 7:145)

Ayat 145 mentions the Ten Commandments.

> And we ordained laws for him in the tablets in all matters, both commanding and explaining all things, (and said): take

---

[122] Zabur 139:7-8

[123] Tawrat, Exodus 3, See also Surah 20:11

[124] Tawrat, Genesis 18:2

[125] Injil, John 1:14

and hold these with firmness, and enjoin thy people to hold fast by the best in the precepts.

Why did Allah give these commandments? To make people righteous before Allah? Sadly, no. Every person, no matter how hard he or she tries, fails to keep the law.

The Injil says, "So then, the law is holy, and the commandment is holy, righteous and good."[126] However, "For the law made nothing perfect."[127] Also the Injil says, "Clearly no one who relies on the law is justified before God, because 'the righteous will live by faith.'"[128] We all fail to keep Allah's law. "…but the people of Israel, who pursued the law as the way of righteousness, have not attained their goal."[129]

Why can't we keep Allah's law? "The mind governed by the flesh is hostile to God; it does not submit to God's law, nor can it do so."[130]

This puts all of us into a very difficult predicament. Allah sent the law of righteousness through Musa. He commands us to worship him alone. He commands us to honor our parents. He condemns theft, deceit and adultery. A perfect man is one who keeps Allah's laws perfectly.

But who can do this? Every human slips up at least once. And that doesn't even include the secret life of the heart. The Injil says, "For whoever keeps the whole law and yet stumbles at just one point is

---

[126] Injil, Romans 7:12

[127] Injil, Hebrews 7:19

[128] Injil, Galatians 3:11

[129] Injil, Romans 9:31

[130] Injil, Romans 8:7

guilty of breaking all of it."[131] Justification through the law is all or nothing. A person would have to keep Allah's law perfectly every minute of every day of his or her life to actually please Allah and avoid condemnation. The slightest disobedience brings complete guilt. In other words, a person is either 100% righteous or 0%. Since we all have inherited a broken heart from our first parents in the Garden of Eden, at some time or another we all break the law, making us 0% righteous. You can keep the law of gravity 99% of the time, but if you break it once by jumping off a cliff, you will certainly die.

Allah's law serves a different purpose than to give us a way to make ourselves righteous. That way is impossible. It is a street marked "dead-end". "No exit". It goes nowhere except darkness. Later we will look more carefully at the real purpose of the law.

Tawrat, Prophets and Injil Foretell Muhammad? (Surah 7:157)

Friends often tell me, "Your books foretell the coming of Muhammad. Musa said a Prophet like him would come. Isa said that another would come after him." They are thinking of passages like Surah 7:15. "Those who follow the Messenger, the unlettered Prophet, whom they find mentioned in their own-in the Law and the Gospel..."

Long before reading the Qur'an I studied the Earlier Books. The story begins with Adam and Hawwa, Nuh, Ibrahim, Musa and then progresses to the kings Davud and Suleiman. The prophet Yahiya came preparing the way for al-Masih. Extraordinary in every way, Isa al-Masih fulfilled dozens of prophecies, some spoken thousands of years before he was born.

After Isa returned to Heaven, his follower Peter clearly marked Isa as the Prophet of whom Musa spoke.

And he shall send Isa al-Masih, which before was preached

---

[131] Injil, James 2:10

unto you: Whom the heaven must receive until the time of restitution of all things, which God hath spoken by the mouth of all his holy prophets since the world began. For Musa truly said unto the fathers, "A prophet shall the Lord your God raise up unto you of your brethren, like unto me; him shall ye hear in all things whatsoever he shall say unto you."

Christians accept Isa al-Masih as the Prophet who Musa prophesied would come later.[132]

What about the Helper who Isa promised to come after he returned to Heaven? Some Muslims think the Injil predicts the coming of Muhammad. The question hinges on the difference between the Greek words, *y* (παράκλητος) or *periklutos* (περικλυτος).[133]

Though Isa likely spoke Aramaic with his friends, the Injil was later written mostly in the common Greek (*Koine*) language. In the Mediterranean region Greek was an international language and very important.

One day Isa spoke with his disciples about the future. He explained that he was physically leaving them. He had lived about 33 years. Still a young man, his time on earth was rapidly passing. Naturally, his friends were frightened and confused. Why would he leave them so early with so much work left to do? Wouldn't he set them free from their Roman overlords? Where was he going? How could they continue without his leadership? Isa comforted them with these words, "I will ask the Father, and he will give you another Helper, to

---

[132] Tawrat, Deuteronomy 18:15. Isa was a prophet and more. He was the heavenly man who died as the sacrificial Lamb of Allah. Like Musa, he led people to freedom.

[133] Injil, John 14

be with you forever."[134]

Isa promised another *paracletos* (παράκλητος), meaning a comforter or helper, "one called alongside to help." Like a best friend, parent or a mentor, he gives comfort with true counsel, strong encouragement and perfect peace.

Hundreds of years passed after Isa. Muhammad became famous and Muslim scholars grew curious. Did the Injil predict his coming? They read the Injil and suggested that Isa promised the coming of the man *Ahmed* (the praised one) instead of a spirit. They claimed the Injil says, "he shall give you another Ahmad" and that the original Injil used the word *periklutos* (περικλυτος) meaning "praised one."[135]

This claim is problematic. First, no ancient or modern copy of the Injil uses the word Ahmad (*periklutos*, περικλυτος). No such Ayat exists anywhere. One of the oldest copies of the Injil is called Papyrus 66. Comparing it with other ancient Injil copies we see no difference. They all say Helper (*paracletos*, παράκλητος). There is no doubt about this.

Second, Isa goes on to describe the Helper as spirit, not human. The Helper continues Isa's work of giving comfort and saving sinners. He is invisible and unknown to the world, but known (not seen) by Isa's followers. He endlessly abides with and in Isa's followers, leading them into all truth. Coming forth from the very essence of Allah, the Helper is therefore not an angel or man.[136]

In other passages the Injil calls the Helper the Holy Spirit. In fact,

---

[134] Injil, John 14:16

[135] Injil, John 14:15

[136] Injil, John 14:16-26

twenty-three different Ayat in the Injil call him the Spirit of al-Masih.

Isa al-Masih told his friends, "And surely I am with you always, to the very end of the age."[137] He physically left them for a season, but as the Helper he spiritually remains right at their side, even abiding in them.

These Ayat in the Injil establish that Isa fulfilled Musa's promise of another Prophet coming after him and that he does not leave his disciples alone, he spiritually remains with them as the Helper (*paracletos*, παράκλητος).

Sometimes my Muslim friends strongly resist. "No! The Tawrat, Prophets and Injil most certainly predict the coming of Muhammad." The conversation goes back and forth.

"Let me ask a question," I respond. "Since you believe the Tawrat, Prophets and Injil are corrupted, why bother trying to find verses in them that predict the coming of Muhammad?"

"Because the Qur'an says the Earlier Books foretell his coming. They must be there."

"Why trust anything in the Tawrat, Prophets and Injil? If they were corrupted, then everything they might have said about Muhammad could be lost. And anyway, since you have the Qur'an, why do you need the Earlier Books?"

This is worth thinking about.

"You're right," someone answers. "I don't need the Tawrat, Prophets and Injil, but maybe parts of it weren't completely corrupted."

"Very interesting. So you realize that some Muslims think that at least parts of the Earlier Books weren't corrupted. We've also seen that the Qur'an respects them, so shouldn't we reconsider the possibility that

---

[137] Injil, Matthew 28:20

none of the Tawrat, Prophets and Injil was ever corrupted?"

If we truly want to know the truth, we must be truthful in our search.

Beautiful Names of Allah (Surah 7:180)

Most Muslims believe there are 99 Beautiful Names of Allah and that memorizing them may give special blessings or even entrance to Paradise. Some people have talked of a hidden 100th name. The old story is that Allah told the 100th name only to the camel, so he smiles and looks down smugly at humans because he knows it and they don't!

These names are understood to show the various attributes of Allah such as his mercy, strength, forgiveness and so forth.

Should we go on a search for the 100th name? What more could we learn? Here is a hint.

One day a devout Muslim girl listened to the message of a famous Imam. At his conclusion she asked, "Teacher, when I stand in the light of Allah's holiness, I see my own sinfulness and disobedience. Can you tell me? Does Allah love sinners? Does Allah love me, a sinner?"

> We love him, because he first loved us.

The teacher studied her face, but could not answer. In his understanding, Allah only loves those who do righteousness. Allah does not love sinners.[138]

In the darkness of moments, when the deepest and most rebellious secrets of the human heart are revealed openly before Allah, how does he respond? Amazingly, we make this discovery. "But God demonstrates his own love for us in this: While we were still sinners,

---

[138] Surah 7:55

Christ died for us."[139] Allah doesn't love us on the condition that we first love him. "We love him because he first loved us."[140] If Allah only loved good people, no one would qualify for his love. He would love no one, because no one is worthy of his love. He loves because of *grace*. If he loves one sinner he loves them all. His love makes no distinctions. Could the 100th name for Allah be Love?

---

[139] Injil, Romans 5:8

[140] Injil, 1 John 4:19

Chapter 8

Surah 8: Al Anfal (The Spoils of War)

What Kind of War? (Surah 8)

Does fighting in the way of Allah have anything to do with life today? At the time of Muhammad and his first followers, physical warfare and hostilities were a part of life. Many people lived by the sword and died by the sword. We need to understand this first of all. Surah 8 talks about physical warfare between Muslims and non-Muslims. Surah 8:12, "I am with you: give firmness to the Believers: I will instill terror into the hearts of the Unbelievers: smite ye above their necks and smite all their fingertips off them."

Why were they fighting? The polytheists were blocking Muslims from entering the "sacred Mosque."[141] Furthermore, they gathered their forces against the Muslims. Surah 8:5 says that some of the believers "disliked" being told to come out of their houses to fight against the

---

[141] Surah 8:34

unbelievers.[142]

How far should the fighting extend? The Tawrat tells me that the children of Ibrahim only fought to protect their limited Promised Land. The battle was limited in space and time. Once they settled the land, the battles ceased. Allah didn't promise to give Ibrahim's people the entire earth. He only promised them a tiny piece. Contrary to earthly expectations, Isa told his followers to lay down their arms and obey the unbelieving rulers.

The concept of countries and governments, like China or Italy, has only existed for a couple of hundred years. During the time of Muhammad, kings and princes ruled their lands. Sometimes they had complex governments, like the ancient China Empire, and sometimes not. The Roman Empire had almost crumbled by the 6th century. Ibrahim's people no longer had government or king. The Greeks were scattered across the Mediterranean. Arab tribes scattered out widely across the Arab peninsula and sometimes fought one another.

In that fractured world, Islam introduced a new Sharia and community (Ummah). They didn't think of themselves as Arab Muslims or Chinese Muslims, there were simply Muslims. They were all expected to follow Muhammad and submit to the Sharia. Slowly the number of tribes that embraced Islam increased until people from many different places and languages became Muslim.

Sometimes Muslims felt threatened by non-Muslims so they took up arms to fight. For example, in the early 8th century North Africa Muslims thought the Goths in Spain posed a threat and were oppressing people living in Spain. They launched a military campaign across the sea and attacked Spain, eventually taking it and establishing the rule of Islam. They moved against southern France in 734 CE with the rationale that the unbelievers in France posed a threat. Failing to

---

[142] Surah 8:5

win against Charles Martel of Tours, they pulled back and established themselves in Spain for hundreds of years.

On the eastern front, Islam spread beyond Arabia, bringing more territory under the control of the Ummah and Caliph. In 1071 CE the Byzantine Empire lost Manzikert to the Seljuk Turks. Two hundred years later the Ottoman Empire arose. Feeling threatened and betrayed by the Byzantines, Fatih Sultan Mehmet struck the final remaining Byzantine stronghold of Constantinople in 1453 CE. The fall of the great walled city to the flag of Islam sealed the dominion of Islam across all of North Africa, Arabia, Central Asia and a large part of the Far East, as well as opening the door to Europe.

"Jihad is always defensive," the Muslim scholar said, becoming very excited. "Christians are wrong to suggest that Islam spread by the sword." I listened, interested to hear his side of the story.

In the discussion about physical jihad against injustice, the point is made that Muslims should never be the aggressor. Fighting is justified as self-defense. Surah 8:39 says, "Fight them on until there is no more tumult or oppression, and there prevail justice and Faith in Allah altogether and everywhere; but if they cease, verily Allah doth see all that they do."

Muslim scholars view the world in two main groups, *Dar al Harb* (House of War) and *Dar al Islam* (House of Islam). Looking at the Islamic conquest of Spain and later Istanbul, I wonder, how do Muslim leaders determine what constitutes a threat to Islam? According to Surah 8:39, the physical struggle against people and places in the Dar al Harb (House of War), must never end until justice and the faith of Islam are universal. Does this mean that the existence of a non-believing civilization or government is in itself a threat to Islam? In other words, is Islam always under threat by non-believers, even if they aren't aggressively attacking Muslims? Does their mere unbelief warrant Muslims to advance against them in order to subdue them and establish faith in Allah, regular prayers and Sharia in the land? Is the best defense a good offense?

I realize these could be awkward questions. It seems that a few people have completely internalized the idea of jihad and say it only means a private attempt to make oneself a better Muslim. I can imagine someone simply saying that Surah 8 doesn't apply in the modern world. But what does that mean? If Surah 8 doesn't apply in the modern world, how does anyone know which parts of the Qur'an apply today and which don't?

I'm sure someone could rightly say to me that I just don't understand. That's entirely possible, and I admit my limitations. But this Surah is not hard to read. There is no mention of the fight limited to a time or place. For people living in any time period, the vital question is what kind of relationship must Muslims pursue with lands ruled by unbelievers?

Chapter 9

Surah 9: Al Tawbah (The Repentance) or Bara'ah (The Disavowal)

Rules for Treaties with Unbelievers (Surah 9:1-29)

History teaches us that during Muhammad's lifetime he participated in at least twenty-seven military campaigns. Notable battles include Badr, Uhud and Trench. On one occasion he was wounded but survived.

At times Muslims made peace agreements with non-Muslims. This passage suggests that treaties are not permanent and that they are to be honored under certain conditions. Surah 9:3-5,

> But when the forbidden months are past, then fight and slay the pagans wherever ye find them, and seize them, beleaguer them, and lie in wait for them in every stratagem (of war); but if they repent, and establish regular Prayers and practise regular Charity, then open the way for them: for Allah is Oft-Forgiving, Most Merciful.

As before, we must first ask if Surah 9 is a command for the Muslim Ummah at all times and places. The Islamic Ummah is not a country or race of people. Under the leadership of Muhammad and then the Caliphs, Muslims made ceasefire agreements with non-Muslims.

Ayat 5 is the most direct command in this section. Does it mean fight polytheists, Jews and Christians (People of the Book) or just the polytheists? Perhaps Jews and Christians are also polytheists, since they are accused of making associates with Allah? In any case, Surah 9:29 expands the scope of battle.

> Fight those who believe not in Allah nor the Last Day, nor hold that forbidden which hath been forbidden by Allah and His Messenger, nor acknowledge the Religion of truth, from among the People of the Book, until they pay the Jizyah with willing submission, and feel themselves subdued.

These Ayat boil down to this basic question. If these Ayat still apply today, does the Qur'an command defensive or offensive fighting or both?

We have considered the examples of Spain and Anatolia. When Islam spreads into a neighboring area, it will encounter unbelievers of all kinds. When some of these unbelievers hear the message of Islam but refuse to accept it, do they pose a threat? If unbelievers try to stop Muslims from establishing their own prayers and mosques, is that a threat?

Ayat 4 describes some unbelievers who kept their agreement with the Muslims. However, the transition between Ayat 4 and 5 makes it unclear what happens after the agreements expire. Are Muslims then expected to again strive in battle to advance the faith?

Some people might reply, "That's all well and true, but of course the 7th century world was vastly different than the 21st century. Everything is more complex and advanced. No one is riding around on camels in the desert anymore, covered in robes to block out the sand and scratching the ground to find a sip of water. We have 4-G internet, heart transplants and interplanetary travel. We need a modern attitude about these ancient writings."

This is partly true. Technology and science have made huge advances. Many humans live longer and more comfortably than ever in history. But at the same time there are still people who live in the desert and scratch out a living as their ancestors have done for thousands of years.

Technology has changed. The world has changed for many people. But has the Qur'an changed? Did it mean something for 7th century people that it doesn't mean today?

I've visited Islamic websites say that Jews, Christians and other unbelievers want to use Surah 9 and similar passages to slander Islam. "Islam is peaceful and never violent. Only enemies of Islam spread lies that Muslims practice violence. They want to hinder people from becoming Muslims."

Sitting with a powerful Islamic leader one afternoon in Asia, I listened to him explain his views on Islam. He sipped coffee and said, "If the news media in America would only show what true, sincere Islam is really like, the entire country would convert to the religion of the prophet Muhammad in one day."

While I don't deny that sometimes people slander other religions and spread lies about beliefs different from their own, I feel the need to consider another possibility about why many people want to know the real meaning of war in both the Earlier Books and in the Qur'an.

What if some people are worried? What if some people are afraid? Is it fair for an honest man, for example, a Canadian, to look at the problems in Sudan, Syria, or Afghanistan and wonder if Muslims living there feel worried or afraid of Jews and Christians oppressing or attacking them? He might find a Jewish friend and ask, "Does your Holy Book tell you to attack and subdue non-Jews?" Richard

Dawkins, perhaps the most famous atheist of the early 21st century, wrote these words,

> The God of the Old Testament is arguably the most unpleasant character in all fiction: jealous and proud of it; a petty, unjust, unforgiving control-freak; a vindictive, bloodthirsty ethnic cleanser; a misogynistic, homophobic, racist, infanticidal, genocidal, filicidal, pestilential, megalomaniacal, sadomasochistic, capriciously malevolent bully.[143]

What will the Jew or Christian, say in reply to Dawkins? Do religions cause violence? I would say, "I understand your concerns, but I don't agree with your conclusion. The violence you see in the Tawrat and Prophets was Allah's just wrath against evil humanity. Furthermore, the story doesn't end with his wrath. It moves on to Isa al-Masih. In his willingness to suffer and die on the cross he proved that Allah loves us. He was willing to enter our suffering and then won the victory over death. The way of Isa revealed in the Injil completely forbids Christian imperialism. Isa's first disciples were men of peace. Almost all died for their faith, yet they forgave their enemies and returned good for evil."

Do the Tawrat, Prophets and Injil lay out a blueprint for mistreating non-Christians? Does the Injil command Christians to "Fight in the way of Isa?" No, Isa told his followers to put away their weapons because his kingdom is spiritual. Richard Dawkins and his unbelieving friends have no reason to fear Isa's followers attacking them.

What should non-Muslims think when they approach passages like Surah 9:29? "Should I be afraid? Will someone try to make me pay a Jizyah? Will they try to make me feel subdued?"

---

[143] Richard Dawkins, *The God Delusion.* Mariner Books; Reprint edition, January 16, 2008.

"The world has never seen such religious freedom like the days of the Osman Muslims," my friend said, motioning with his hand at all the great mosques and churches that stood beside us. "Jews, Christians and Muslims lived together in perfect peace, each practicing their own religion without any fear. Didn't civilization flourish under the rule of Islam, while Europe went through the long Dark Ages? Islam is the most tolerant religion ever."

History shows how Islamic rule often worked. Jews and Christians could live under the rule of Muslims as *dhimmis*, non-Muslims minorities. Here's a sample list of conditions put upon the non-Muslims.

· All non-Muslim males had to pay a poll-tax (jizyah) to the Muslim state as an expression of their submission to Muslim rule. (Many documents say they should experience some kind of humiliation while making the payment - e.g. by being struck on the neck.) If they owned land, they also had to pay a land tax (kharaj).

· Non-Muslims could not engage in military service, since this would involve them in jihad, Holy War.

· Jews and Christians were not allowed to build new churches or synagogues or repair those in areas occupied by Muslims.

· They were not allowed to display the cross outside churches or to hold public religious processions outside.

· Their houses could not be built taller than those of Muslims.

· Their clothes should be different from the clothes worn by Muslims. Often they had to wear a badge to mark them out from Muslims, and sometimes they were required to shave their heads.

· They were forbidden to ride on horses, and had to ride on mules or donkeys.

· They must show respect to Muslims - for instance by giving up their seats to them.[144]

With stone church buildings crumbling, public humiliation and no participation in government, wouldn't the Jewish and Christian communities naturally grow weaker, if not eventually wither altogether?

The situation in Arabia has always been much stricter. Non-Muslims were completely banned from ever entering Mecca. Caliph Umar fulfilled Muhammad's command that two religions not remain in the Arab peninsula by issuing an edict for all non-Muslims to leave. To this day, the Islamic House of Saud maintains strict control over the land, insuring that only one religion can and ever will officially exist there.[145]

Considering all this, how might a Christian feel when he or she reads Surah 9? How would anyone feel when being caught between two difficult choices? If the person chooses to live as a dhimmi it implies inferiority and submission to the ruling class. If he or she chooses to become a Muslim only to avoid dhimmi status, it means fake religion, changing their faith only for worldly gain.

A modern Muslim says, "That's all silly, you are talking about life from the dark ages. In the 21st century we are enlightened, we believe in democracy. It's enough simply to be a human. We make no distinction based on religion." This may sound progressive, but opinions are like

---

144 Colin Chapman, *Cross and Crescent, IVP* Books; 02 edition, February 28, 2008.

145 Since the arrival of oil wealth, hundreds of thousands of non-Muslims have been hired for the working class in Gulf countries. Many of these are Christians from Asia who can practice their religion under strict laws.

feathers in the wind while the words of ancient books are like great stones.

The Oldest Copies of the Qur'an

No one has an original Qur'an written by Muhammad himself. In fact, history says that Muhammad could not read or write. It is believed that the angel Jibril spoke the Qur'an to Muhammad who recited the Ayat to his followers. They in turn memorized the words. Eventually they began to write down the Ayat on different materials like wood and parchment. History says that Uthman ordered all copies of the Qur'an be burned except the version that he officially endorsed. The Uthman version was considered the standard. Almost all variations were destroyed.

What happened after that? Muslim scribes made more copies of the Qur'an. Early copies are recognized by their style of Arabic writing. These styles include *Makkan, Mashq, Hijāzī* and *Kufic.* Scholars use the styles to determine what century the manuscript was written.

One of the oldest copies of the Qur'an can be found in the Topkapi Palace of Istanbul and another of the oldest copies in Tashkent, Uzbekistan. These copies written on vellum pages date to around the 8th or 9th centuries. In 2015 an even older copy of the Qur'an was discovered that dates back to the very first days of Islam.

Dozens of partial ancient Qur'an copies still exist. These are carefully preserved and studied. Scholars have detected some variations between the copies. There is no single original Qur'an. In 1924 the standard Egyptian *Hafs* Qur'an edition was published.[146]

---

[146] "Preserving and protecting the Qur'an", Ummah, "Comparing the Egyptian edition to the oldest available Qur'an, the Tashkent Qur'an, will show that there have been many human errors in the Tashkent Qur'an that has to be corrected when the Egyptian edition was made. The errors were obvious because the Qur'an has always

Interestingly, after comparing many ancient copies of the Qur'an with one another, Muslim scholars have come to say exactly what many Christians have learned about the Injil: although there are some variations in the ancient texts, the essential message is unaltered.

> Opinions are like feathers in the wind while the words of ancient books are like great stones.

Why Fight the Jews and Christians? (Surah 9:30-31)

So far I have seen nothing in the Qur'an that commands Muslims to fight unless they have a cause considered just under Sharia law. The underlying belief is that Islam alone provides a just society and the correct religion. The Qur'an teaches that Islam alone ends evil and injustice (like killing newborn girls), and false religion, like idolatry.

But why are Jews and Christian accused of idolatry?[147] Surah 9:30 explains, "The Jews call Uzair a son of Allah, and the Christians call Christ the son of Allah."

Reading this the first time I felt surprised. Having studied the Tawrat and Prophets since my youth, I knew that devout Jews are strict

---

been completely memorized and kept in its oral transmission to these days and can be verified against any written book. It is impossible to consider that God meant to preserve and protect the written books for example by Uthman (the Tashkent Qur'an), or any other human being for this matter when they are full of human errors. God's promise is to provide the mean to verify any written Qur'an against what He has in the Master tablets as we see in 85:21-22." http://www.ummah.com/forum/showthread.php?66079-Is-the-Qur'an-preserved, accessed February 2018.

[147] My point is the Tawrat, Prophets and Injil absolutely condemned idolatry. Idolaters could not be Jews or Christians.

monotheists.[148] They declare, "Hear O Isra'il, the Lord your One."[149] They couldn't imagine worshipping anyone as a son of Allah. To the contrary, they would stone people to death for making such blasphemy.

The Injil gives some of the best evidence for this. One day Isa spoke about himself to the religious leaders. He made the audacious claim, "I and the Father are one." The leaders became enraged and started gathering stones for certain execution.[150] Isa asked, "For which of my good works do you stone me?" They said they would stone him not for his good works but for his blasphemy of making himself out to be one with Allah. In other words, they were saying to him, "your works are good, but your words are bad."

Five hundred years after Isa the Qur'an says that some Jews were calling Uzair the son of Allah. We don't know everything about the Jewish communities scattered across Arabia in the 6th century. Who worshipped Uzair? We don't know. But one thing we do know for sure, if the other Jews discovered them worshipping someone called Uzair, they would have done the same thing they tried to do to Isa. They would have taken up stones to kill them. Pious Jews had zero tolerance for blasphemy! They had to confess Allah is One.

The Jews and the Qur'an condemn blasphemy. That still leaves the question of Isa. Were Christians guilty of blasphemy? As we have

---

[148] Among some non-religious Jewish communities, as many as 60% are atheists. They are thoroughly secular in thought.

[149] See Injil, Matthew 22

[150] Injil, John 10:30-33, Jesus said, "'I and the Father are one.' Again his Jewish opponents picked up stones to stone him, but Jesus said to them, 'I have shown you many good works from the Father. For which of these do you stone me?' 'We are not stoning you for any good work,' they replied, 'but for blasphemy, because you, a mere man, claim to be God.'" They did not care what the Romans would do to them even if they stoned Isa.

seen, that depends on who Isa truly was, not just opinions about him. If Isa was no more than other men, a creature of the dust with a spirit created by Allah, then Christians are guilty of blasphemy. It would be the same if Christians called a tree the son of Allah or a mountain the daughter of Allah. If someone worships anything created by Allah and considers it equal to or a part of Allah, he or she is guilty of blasphemy. There is an absolute difference between the eternal Allah and temporal creation in their essential natures.

Fake Believers (Surah 9:56)

During the first century of Islam, the Qur'an called many Muslims into battle against non-Muslims. But battle is hard and dangerous, making some people want to hide in their safe home. The Qur'an frowns on these people. In 9:56 it even warns that some Muslims were not sincere. They were fake believers. "They swear by Allah that they are indeed of you; but they are not of you: yet they are afraid." Over the centuries the question often arises, who is a true Muslim? What makes a true Muslim? The Shahada? The name Muslim? Surah 9:56 shows that even making an oath by Allah is no proof of real faith. If not, is it still a problem today that some people who call themselves Muslims are in fact self-deceived?

A New Enemy Introduced (Surah 9:73)

The Qur'an considers polytheists, some Jewish people and some Christians as enemies, because of their injustice and unbelief. Surah 9:73 introduces a new enemy. "O Prophet! strive hard against the Unbelievers and the Hypocrites, and be firm against them. Their abode is Hell- an evil refuge indeed."

Who are these hypocrites (*Munafiqun*, المنافقون(ال)? Surah 9:74 says that they committed blasphemy after accepting Islam, plotted against

Muhammad, and lied about it.[151] They did all these things after receiving a share of the loot from Muhammad. They also didn't give as much to charity as they promised.

What does the Qur'an say will happen to hypocrites? Surah 9:74, "Allah will punish them with a grievous penalty in this life and in the Hereafter: they shall have none on earth to protect or help them."

Following their Leader (Surah 9:86-88)

These Ayat show that Muhammad was a military leader. His followers were instructed to strive and fight alongside him. Faced with the prospect of injury or death in battle, some powerful people found excuses to avoid pain. They stayed home.

> When a Surah comes down, enjoining them to believe in Allah and to strive and fight along with His Messenger, those with wealth and influence among them ask thee for exemption, and say: "Leave us: we would be with those who sit." They prefer to be with who remain behind: their hearts are sealed and so they understand not.

The injured, sick or poor have a right to stay at home and not fight. Sometimes there were not enough horses for everyone to ride into battle, so some fighters had to stay behind, but they were very disappointed they couldn't ride with the army.

Fake Mosques (Surah 9:107-110)

Not only did some hypocrites lie, blaspheme and refuse to fight for Islam, we see here that some shamelessly built mosques to "disunite the believers." Ayat 97 says "The Arabs of desert are the worst in

---

[151] Surah 9:74, "They swear by Allah that they said nothing (evil), but indeed they uttered blasphemy, and they did it after accepting Islam; and they meditated a plot which they were unable to carry out: this revenge of theirs was (their) only return for the Bounty with which Allah and His Messenger had enriched them!"

unbelief and hypocrisy."

We see here that not all people who call themselves Muslims are always the same and not all mosques are necessarily the same.

As a Christian reading through the Surah, I am not qualified to say what group of Muslims is the purest. I have Sunni friends and Shia friends, friends from Alevi background and Sufi friends. A Sunni friend once told me that Muslims in northern Nigeria, people like Boko Haram, are not genuine Muslims. I assume he meant that they do not live and fight in the true way of Allah and his Messenger. I asked him where I could find true Muslims and he said he thinks there are some living deep in the Anatolian mountains.

Surah 9 teaches that there are non-Muslims like polytheists, Jews and Christians, and there are lazy Muslims who don't like to fight because it isn't comfortable, and there are hypocrites who swear and call themselves Muslims, but who really don't believe. From my point of view, it seems that identifying a Christian or a polytheist would be easier than deciding who is a real Muslim and who is a hypocritical one. Anyway, it's not up to me to decide.

It is interesting to notice that just as not all Muslims are the same, neither is everyone who calls himself a Christian. I've met "Christians" living in Europe who have never read the Injil and are not sure if they believe in a Creator. They inherited religion from their ancestors. They have religious buildings and holidays, but no personal faith. Some of these people wear a golden cross on a chain. Some of them point to the sky and say, "Thank Allah," but if you ask them where Isa was born, they would only stare blankly. For these people, being a Christian means they can eat pork, drink wine and confess their sins to a priest. According to Isa, these things have no power to raise someone from the dead and give eternal life.

One day Isa's disciples complained that many people following him were hypocrites. Isa said that true believers and hypocrites would increase together, like weeds and wheat growing side by side in the fields. He told them to leave the hypocrites alone, lest they accidentally pull up the wheat with the weeds. On the last day, Allah himself will separate the wheat and weeds.[152]

How Great is Allah's Kindness? (Surah 9:113)

Our journey now carries us into a very sensitive subject. Is there a limit to Allah's kindness? "It is not fitting, for the prophet and those who believe, that they should pray for forgiveness for Pagans, even though they be of kin, after it is clear to them that they are companions of the Fire."

In Ayat 114 we read that Ibrahim prayed for Allah to forgive his very own father, a polytheist. But when he did not repent and become a friend of Allah, Ibrahim departed.

Before talking about the limits to Allah's kindness toward sinful people, let's think about the subject of prayer. What happens when people pray? Prayer is often understood as reciting certain words before Allah. Regular prayers (*salat*) have a fixed routine. We don't see Ibrahim recite memorized prayers, but instead we see him talking with Allah from his heart.

Now the sensitive question. When does Allah stop showing kindness to sinful people? Ayat 113-114 say that Allah's kindness stops "after it is clear" that a person is a companion of fire. Some people think this is only after people die without accepting Islam. Maybe, but the Ayat shows that Ibrahim stopped praying for his father while he was still alive.

Surah 9:80 gives more insight. It says, "if thou ask seventy times for their forgiveness, Allah will not forgive them: because they have rejected Allah and His Messenger." Is this verse talking about praying

---

[152] Injil, Matthew 13:30

for Allah to forgive the companions of fire? How many kind and merciful invitations to accept Islam should a non-Muslim receive before he or she must be handed over to their unbelief? Ayat 80 says that praying 70 times is a waste because Allah will not extend mercy to those unbelievers.

Sometimes people mock the hope that Isa al-Masih will come again. Even in the time of his first followers mockers arose. But Allah has good reasons for waiting. The Injil says, "The Lord is not slow in keeping his promise, as some understand slowness. Instead he is patient with you, not wanting anyone to perish, but everyone to come to repentance."[153]

When the Romans crucified Isa, they also crucified two thieves, one on his right and one on his left. At first both men in their misery and shame hurled insults and curses at Isa. No doubt they had already heard about Isa, whose fame had spread across Kudus and the countryside. Quiet as a lamb and yet strong as a lion, Isa never returned evil for evil. He forgave his persecutors and killers. Seeing Isa demonstrate divine love while he suffered immense pain and injustice, one of the thieves began to soften. He realized his own unworthiness. Finally, weak from blood loss and exhaustion, the pitiful man said, "Isa, remember me when you come into your kingdom." Isa replied, "Today you will be with me in Paradise."[154]

Isa's example teaches that Allah's loving mercy and kindness wait until the last second, until the last breath is drawn. Over and over, he reaches out to the sinner, inviting him to come home. But even so, a time will come when Allah turns the sinner over to the hardness of his heart.

---

[153] Injil, 2 Peter 3:9

[154] Injil, Luke 23:43

Chapter 10

Surah 10: Yunus

The Straight Way (Surah 10:25)

Surah 10 announces more warnings and promises. Some people believe and do works of righteousness and others disbelieve and live for this world only. Surah 10:8 says their judgment is terrible, an "abode of fire."

All people, good or bad, seem to be searching for something. Perhaps a person is searching for something as simple as bread and water. Someone else searches for love and affection. Another for wealth and power. Some earnestly look for good ways to please Allah so they can escape the fires of Hell and enter Paradise.

This universal searching sends people down many paths. Not all lead to the same place. Speaking of the Straight Way, Ayat 25 says, "But Allah doth call to the home of peace: he doth guide whom he pleaseth to a way that is straight."

A straight line doesn't bend to the right or left. It implies justice and goodness. It is not swayed by difficulty or luxury. A man walking the straight path must be without partiality and without selfishness.

Pathways also lead somewhere. They have a destination. One evening some of Isa's disciples listened to him describe the afterlife. He said he was leaving them physically, but he would prepare a Heavenly mansion for them then return to take them home. The Injil teaches that Heaven is Allah's home. It is like a fabulous city filled with the very presence of Allah. In Allah's presence his people will enjoy praising and worshipping him forever.

Isa's friend Tomas, known for a desire to see the hard facts, asked,

> "Lord, we don't know where you are going, so how can we know the way?" Jesus answered, "I am the way and the truth and the life. No one comes to the Father except through me. If you really know me, you will know my Father as well. From now on, you do know him and have seen him.[155]

Isa said other peculiar things like this about himself: "I am the light of the world." "I am the door." "I am the Good Shepherd." "I am the resurrection and the life." "I am the true vine." "I am the way."[156]

I can appreciate that Surah 10:25 talks about the Straight Way. Every human has a "way of life." Not all these lifestyles are equal. There are two main paths in the world today. The first way has a broad entrance and a wide path. Multitudes travel down this path that leads to destruction. The second path is has a small entrance and follows a narrow way. Only a few find this way, but it leads to eternal life.

Prophetic Books (Surah 10:37-40)

---

[155] Injil, John 14:5-7

[156] These are the "I am" statements of Isa, recorded by his disciple John in the Injil.

Muhammad challenged people accusing him of falsehood. Ayat 38, "Or do they say, he forged it? say: bring then a Surah like unto it." Muhammad built a defense that no human could ever write even one verse of the Qur'an. He argued that the Qur'an is miraculous. Ayat 37, "This Qur'an is not such as can be produced by other than Allah."

I'm not going to argue here whether or not the Qur'an is miraculous. First I want to carefully read through the entire Qur'an, listening to what it has to say.

Having lived in many countries in my lifetime, I am familiar with several other religions and other books claiming to have come from Allah. In Central Asia some of my Muslim neighbors highly respected a famous *tayup*. He could fill a football stadium with 20,000 people. His followers believed he could heal sicknesses and speak life-giving words. They didn't call him a prophet, but they believed he was someone special sent by Allah.

In 1830 a man named Joseph Smith from New York published a book called the *Book of Mormon*. He taught his followers that the Tawrat, Prophets and Injil had been corrupted and that a resurrected prophet named Moroni guided him to secret golden tablets containing a fresh revelation from Allah. Many people rejected his message but his followers multiplied and they made something like a hijrah pilgrimage to a new land near the Great Salt Lake in America. Today millions of people around the world follow Joseph Smith's teachings and the *Book of Mormon*.

Just after I graduated from the university I got a letter from an organization offering me a free copy of *The Urantia Book*. Their website claimed, "*The Urantia Book*, first published by Urantia Foundation in 1955, presents us with the origin, history, and destiny of humanity."[157]

---

[157] "A Brief Description of *The Urantia Book*", https://www.urantia.org/urantia-book, accessed February 2018.

"Why would I need their book to tell me that?" I thought. "Doesn't the Tawrat, Prophets and Injil already show us all those things?"

In 1879 a somewhat secretive new religious group started in North America which became known as the Jehovah's Witnesses. They grew into several million people worldwide by the 21st century. They didn't publish a new holy book like Joseph Smith, but a team of their writers and editors sat down and made critical changes in the Tawrat, Prophets and Injil. They called their altered version of the Earlier Books the *New World Translation*. When Muslim friends tell me the Earlier Books have been corrupted, they are correct if they specifically mean the Jehovah's Witness version. Imagine a Christian printing his own translation of the Qur'an and making small but critical changes. Anyone with a computer and printer can make a counterfeit book far more easily then they can make counterfeit money.

Looking around the world, we see that the Hindus have their holy books, called the *Vedas*. The Buddhists read the *Tripitaka* to follow their master Buddha, whom they consider the *Enlightened One* or *Awakened One*.

Hundreds of years after the Qur'an came, Guru Nanak started the new Sikh religion in India. They revere the *Guru Granth Sahib*, a unique mixture of Islam and Hinduism. Going much farther than the Sikhs in trying to keep everyone happy, the Bahais believe that there are many manifestations of Allah. They believe The Báb and Bahá'u'lláh came after Muhammad. The Bab said, "O Thou who art the first to believe in Me! Verily, I say, I am the Báb, the Gate of God."[158] Considered a heretic by the Muslims, The Bab was executed on July 9, 1850. Likewise, many of his followers suffered imprisonment and execution.

---

[158] "The coming of the Báb", BBC,
http://www.bbc.co.uk/religion/religions/bahai/history/bab_1.shtml, accessed February 2018.

I don't have space here to go on. On every continent and in every age we can find people claiming prophethood and the books they wrote. Honestly, it can get very confusing! Why believe anything?

My wife and I once visited Kudus to see where the children of Ibrahim and al-Masih lived. Today Kudus is a bustling city with both ancient and ultra-modern sections. After having coffee we walked down a narrow street in the Muslim quarter of the city. Beautiful archways and honey-colored walls lined the narrow alleyways. Some playful Arab boys ran out to meet us. They quickly noticed we looked different and approached us suspiciously. We smiled at them and I said in Arabic, "*Asalamawlekum.*" Suddenly they stopped and smiled back at us. Passing downhill we came to the base of the Al Aksa mosque and studied the temple foundations built during King Suleiman's reign.

We walked back to our small hostel at the Jaffa gate, but first we stopped by the traditional burial place of Isa. Every color, shape and size of human being stood in the stone courtyard. It was a somber place.

Was it the actual tomb where Isa's friends put his dead body or did they bury him some other place? I don't know. But I know one thing for sure. No one has ever found his body. Just as the angels asked his friends on the third morning, "Why do you look for the living among the dead?"[159]

"Show us some proof!" Everyone likes proof. No one just gives trust away for free. We need confidence. The Jewish leaders who tested Isa were no different. They demanded, "Show us a sign!" Isa replied, "For as Yunus was three days and three nights in the belly of a huge fish, so the Son of Man will be three days and three nights in the heart

---

[159] Injil, Luke 24:5

of the earth."[160]

Can we find ultimate proof? With the internet I've watched some astonishing magic tricks. Some illusionists have become so good, they appear to defy physical laws, frightening me. My brain tells me that it's only an illusion but my eyes tell me it's a miracle. Still, these are only tricks. They would not withstand scientific scrutiny.

Some people accuse Isa of doing magic tricks. But he said that the most important sign, the only one that really matters as proof, is his resurrection from the dead. If someone could completely give the illusion of dying and rising from the dead three days later, he or she would be the greatest magician of all. After the stone rolled away from the tomb, his disciples saw him alive. The Jewish leaders frantically searched for his missing body. If they could have just found Isa's corpse we wouldn't be talking about him like this today. For two thousand years people have desperately tried to find his bones, hoping to silence the Injil once for all. Yet the resurrection of Isa persistently declares the ultimate miracle proving his message.

We actually don't know how the words of the Qur'an sounded when Muhammad first recited them. The first written copies of the Qur'an did not contain vowel points. Without the vowel points, a word could be pronounced in many different ways. A different pronunciation could make a different word with a different meaning. In centuries after Muhammad, scholars added vowel points to the Qur'an, but they had to make a guess since there were no recordings of Muhammad's voice in the 7th century.[161]

Since no one knows exactly how Muhammad recited the words of the Qur'an, Muslims have traditionally depended heavily upon the *Tafsir*.

---

[160] Injil, Matthew 12:40

[161] This is why there are different readings of the Qur'an in different branches of Islam.

Without the Tafsir commentaries, parts of the Qur'an would be almost beyond comprehension. This makes it harder to make a comment about the quality of the Qur'an's sound and the meaning of the original text.

This brings us to a deeper question, does Surah 10:38 mean that the sound of the Arabic verses are miraculous and without equal (like poetry sounds beautiful with rhymes and rhythms) or does it mean that the message is miraculous or both? I would guess that most people think that both the sound and message of the Qur'an are miraculous. That leads us back to the issue that over a billion Muslims can listen to the Qur'an but not understand what they are hearing. So the sound and the message for many Muslims is disconnected.

I lived in Cyprus for a while, just down the street from a Greek Orthodox Church. How surprised I was one day to hear the local priest chanting over the loudspeakers in ancient Greek. I guessed he was chanting parts of the Injil, but I don't know for sure. In any case, my Greek neighbors confessed to me in private that they didn't understand the priest much better than I! They could hear the chanted words, which they considered beautiful, but they were ignorant of the message.

A similar situation went on for hundreds of years among Roman Catholics. The priests spoke in Latin. Who could understand? Not the common people. It all sounded high, exalted and mystical, but was impractical for their daily lives.

Allah never planned to use unintelligible languages to communicate his love to humans. That's not communication. When Allah's Spirit came like tongues of fire upon Isa's disciples, they miraculously began speaking languages they had never learned. The visitors in Kudus who heard them exclaimed, "we hear them speaking in our heart languages!"[162] Today the world has over 20,000 languages spoken by humans. Allah knows them all.

Nuh's Ark (Surah 10:73)

Evil spread like pestilence through the earth after the days of Adam, driven by the hungry seed of sin growing deeply in the heart. Allah could have justly destroyed everything, but he showed mercy on the human race by saving Nuh's family in the Ark. Surah 10:73,

> They rejected him, but we delivered him, and those with him, in the Ark and we made them inherit while we overwhelmed in the flood those who rejected our Signs. Then see what was the end of those who were warned.

Truly they came to a bleak moment in human history, yet Allah gave a glimmer of light.

The Ark of Nuh, like many stories found in the Tawrat, is a picture of Allah's promised salvation through al-Masih. No one enjoys the Ark more than children. They can play for hours with a toy Ark. They march little pairs of exotic lions, elephants, hippopotamuses and monkeys into the ark and shut the door. The Ark represents hope in the midst of destruction.

Just as the Ark carried eight people safely through the flood waters, al-Masih promises to carry his followers safely through the grave. Just as Nuh and his family put their lives into the Ark, the disciples of Isa put themselves by faith into the resurrection of Isa. The Ark survived the flood and with it so did Nuh and his family. Isa survived death and the grave and along with him so do his trusting followers. Resurrection is his sign.

Ask the People of the Book (Surah 10:94)

---

[162] Injil, Acts 2:8

Again the Qur'an affirms the Earlier Books. The Qur'an says that anyone with doubts about Allah should ask help from the Jews and Christians who read the Earlier Books. Surah 10:94,

> If thou wert in doubt as to what we have revealed unto thee, then ask those who have been reading the book from before thee: the truth hath indeed come to thee from thy Lord: so be in no wise of those in doubt.

Chapter 11

Surah 11: Hud (The Prophet Hud)

If you my Muslim friend are still reading this book with me—and I hope so—we have come a long way. The Surahs now gradually start to get shorter until Surah 114 at the end. I can't comment on everything I read and still keep this book a manageable length, but I want to respond honestly to special ideas I notice along the way.

What is Grace? (Surah 11:3)

Several times we have encountered the concept of grace. The Arabic word فَضْلِه is sometimes translated *fazilet*. In Ayat 3 we read *fazilet* is given to those who show it. The Injil uses the words *charis* (χάρις) and *agape* (ἀγάπη) to express the idea of grace.

True grace is different from a reward or payment. True grace is not merely an act of mercy, when punishment is withheld. True grace showers love and blessing upon someone completely unworthy.

Early one morning long ago a vineyard owner went into town and hired some workers. They agreed to work for regular wages. Later that morning he went again and hired more. Still needing more workers, he went again at noon and again at three and five. As the sun set that evening, all the workers came for their wages. But then the owner gave everyone the same amount of money.

The first workers protested, "What are you doing? We worked long, hot hours. These guys have only been here a couple of hours."

The owner replied, "I'm not being unfair to you, friend. Take your pay and go. I want to give the one who was hired last the same as I gave you. Don't I have the right to do what I want with my own money? Or are you envious because I am generous?"[163]

My sister spoke to me one day about this story. "I used to complain that this didn't seem fair. How can the owner pay everyone the same amount? But then I realized that this is a story about Allah's grace. It's a gift, freely given and freely accepted."

Allah owns a vineyard. All the earth is his field. He places humans in it to work. Some try to do good more than others, but none can work as well as the vineyard owner. Anything Allah gives to us is more than we deserve.

Sara's Laugher (Surah 11:71)

Discord entered Ibrahim's life through his bad decisions. Allah promised him a son and that through his family line salvation would come to all the nations.

Hajar was a slave woman. Sara was free and Ibrahim's lawful wife. Ayat 71 refers to the story in the Tawrat when holy guests came to Ibrahim's tent to dine with his family.

The Lord asked Ibrahim, "Where is Sara?"

---

[163] Injil, Matthew 20:1-16

"Inside the tent," Ibrahim said.

Allah then promised that Sara would become pregnant with a son. Inside the tent, Sara laughed. How could it be? She and Ibrahim were old and wrinkled.

> The genealogies leave a trail of evidence that we can follow back over the years step by step from Isa to Davud to Isak and Ibrahim.

Later the guests asked her why she laughed. Frightened, she denied laughing. But Allah said, "Yes, you did laugh." Months later their son was born. Just as Allah had instructed, they named him Isak, which means laughter. Isak was the son of the covenant and through him would come the *Seed* of salvation.[164]

The Tawrat and Injil carefully record several genealogies of Adam, Ibrahim, Isak, Ismail, Yakup, Yusuf, Musa and Davud all the way to Isa. The lists are long and detailed.[165]

Why? Why all the trouble? These genealogies confirm that Isa was the Seed of salvation. They leave a trail of evidence that we can follow back over the years step by step from Isa to Davud to Isak and Ibrahim.

When Sara laughed at the thought of a son, little could she have imagined how much joyful laughter Allah would give people through his grace in Isa al-Masih?

---

[164] Tawrat, Genesis 17:19

[165] See Injil, Matthew 1; Injil, Luke 3

Chapter 12

Surah 12: Yusuf

Stories to Instruct (Surah 12)

I have discovered that the Qur'an shares many stories with the Tawrat and Injil. Ayat 111 says these stories are "instruction for men endued with understanding." I would agree.

Surah 12 lays out one of the longest stories in the Qur'an. Yusuf's brothers sold him into slavery in Egypt, his master's wife tried to seduce him and falsely accused him, his master threw him into prison and then Allah raised Yusuf to supreme leadership in the Pharaoh's court. Several years later a famine hit the Mediterranean basin, driving his hungry brothers to Egypt in search of food. Little did they know that Allah had raised Yusuf to great power. Yusuf made peace with his brothers and along with Yakup they all moved to Egypt.

We can discover more dramatic details about Yusuf's story in the Tawrat.[166] Yakup gave Yusuf a multi-colored robe of great beauty. His

---

[166] Tawrat, Genesis 37-39

brothers grew fiercely jealous of Yusuf's coat and his dreams predicting that someday they would all bow to him. One day Yakup sent Yusuf into the wilderness to check on his brothers and the flocks. Seeing their opportunity, they plotted to kill him, but the oldest brother Reuben intervened, hoping to rescue Yusuf out of love for his father. Judah, another brother, suggested selling Yusuf for silver. So instead of killing Yusuf they threw him into a pit and waited.

Reuben returned to the pit too late. His brothers had already sold him to a band of Ismaili traders.

Once in Egypt Yusuf went into the household service of a high official named Potiphar. Under Yusuf's wise leadership his household flourished. Seeing his skill and handsomeness, Potiphar's wife became obsessed with lust. Yusuf resisted temptation, but Potiphar accepted his wife's accusations and threw Yusuf into prison.

For years he languished in the darkness. One day he correctly interpreted the dreams of the royal cupbearer and baker who were imprisoned with him. Sadly, the cupbearer forgot Yusuf when he was released from prison.

A dream deeply disturbed the Pharaoh and he demanded someone interpret it for him. The cupbearer suddenly remembered Yusuf in prison and advised the ruler to seek his help.

In the great throne room, Yusuf told the Pharaoh that his dream of healthy and sickly cows warned of a coming famine. His supernatural wisdom made such a deep impression on the Pharaoh that he appointed him to the highest post in the land.

When the famine swept away everything in the region, only Egypt had adequate stores of grain to survive. Yusuf's brothers came pleading for help lest they all die.

Yusuf wept when he made peace with his brothers. They were fearful that he would punish them severely. Yet he showed grace and said,

"You intended to harm me, but God intended it for good to accomplish what is now being done, the saving of many lives.[167]

Like Nuh's Ark, Yusuf's life is a picture of someone greater. The picture shows a man specially loved by his father, clothed with a unique robe of honor, betrayed by his brothers, sold for silver, accused of sin unjustly, buried in a dark prison, raised to life in the highest seat in the land, reconciled to his enemies and offering salvation to many people. Someone wonderful.

---

[167] Tawrat, Genesis 50:20

Chapter 13

Surah 13: Al Ra'd (The Thunder)

In the Beginning (Surah 13:16)

Albert Einstein, the great physicist, could hardly believe his ears. Another scientist named Hubble reported looking through a telescope and finding evidence that the universe is expanding. Einstein and many others in the early 20th century believed the universe existed eternally, with no beginning or end. Suddenly Hubble gave evidence that the universe had a beginning. If it had a beginning, what existed before it?

With more and more powerful instruments, scientists have learned that the universe has about 100 billion galaxies and 70 billion trillion stars. In between these countless stars are billions of light-years of space. They say if we could turn back time 13 billion years, all these stars would be packed closer and closer together. At a precise moment in the past, everything was found in one tiny package. Like a campfire, it ignited and spread out, making the universe we have today.

How was the campfire lit? Where did its firewood grow? This is the question that people have asked themselves since the beginning of humanity. Was it nothing? Was it something? Luck? Perhaps someone?

The Tawrat faces this question unashamedly. "In the beginning, Allah created the heaven and the earth."[168] Suleiman wrote, "By wisdom the Allah laid the earth's foundations, by understanding he set the heavens in place."[169] By his "hand" Allah stretched out the heavens like a tent.[170]

The Qur'an Surah 13:16 says, "or do they assign to Allah partners who have created as he has created, so that the creation seemed to them similar? say: Allah is the Creator of all things: he is the one, the supreme and irresistible." The Tawrat and Qur'an agree that there is only one Creator. False gods do not exist and therefore do not create anything.

Allah is spirit and has no body. What does the prophet mean that "by wisdom" and his "hand" the Lord created? Or consider, why does the Injil say that Allah created the universe with his Word?[171]

Here is a key to this puzzle. How does an artist create a sculpture? The idea originates in his or her mind and is then expressed through talented hands. The greatest Artist, the creative Lord, brought forth His Word and "in him were all things created, in the heavens and upon the earth."[172]

Tawhid is probably the most basic idea in Islam. It means Allah is One (*Al-Ahad*) and Single (*Al-Wahid*). People have many ideas about Tawhid. Connected to this issue people also ask, is the Qur'an eternal

---

[168] Tawrat, Genesis 1:1

[169] Prophets, Proverbs 3:19

[170] Prophets, Yeshaya 40:22

[171] Injil, 2 Peter 3:5

[172] Injil, Colossians 1:16. Even the Qur'an uses this imagery, Surah 15:26, 27, 26 "We created man from sounding clay, from mud moulded into shape;"

or created? If it is eternal, what makes it different from Allah? Would that compromise Tawhid? And how can anything other than Allah be non-created? It is a little uncomfortable to think about Tawhid and talk about an uncreated Qur'an.

In any case, true religion teaches that in the beginning the One and only Allah created everything through his Word. The Word is with Allah and the Word is Allah. To suggest otherwise is like saying a human can live without his or her soul. The soul is with the person and the soul is the person. The Word is One, absolutely integrated in perfect unity.

This is why the Injil says, "Through him all things were made; without him nothing was made that has been made."[173] The Word is not a partner or associate of Allah. The Word does not create an alternate universe. The Word is not in competition with Allah. The eternal Word, through creation, brings glory to the Creator. Christians agree, anyone who says that a god other than Allah has the power to create is in darkness.

More Judgment (Surah 13)

Much of the rest of Al Ra'd speaks of reward for those who follow Muhammad and punishment and Hell for those who do not. As in other Ayat, Muhammad points to the Qur'an as proof of his prophethood. Whenever the unbelievers questioned or criticized his message, he argued that his speech was far superior to anyone else. The warnings of penalties, curses, and punishments for the unbelievers are sometimes ambiguous. Do the Ayat mean that unbelievers will be punished in this world or in Hell or both? Do these warnings frighten unbelievers? Did some people become Muslims in order to escape Hell with its boiling waters and ceaseless fires of torment?

---

[173] Injil, John 1:3

Chapter 14

Surah 14: Ibrahim

A Messenger in Arabic (Surah 14:4)

"We sent not a messenger except in the language of his people, in order to make clear to them."

Born an Arab in the Quraysh tribe, Muhammad spoke the Arabic language, which had been around for at least a thousand years before his birth. Arabs settled in the Arab peninsula and lived as nomads and traders. Life was very harsh in the wind-blasted deserts. Rain rarely fell and grass was precious.

Ayat 4 takes us back to the question about the Qur'an's origin. If Muhammad spoke the Qur'an using 7th century Arabic, the "language of his people", how is it a Heavenly language? The Arabic language slowly developed over hundreds of years. Furthermore the Qur'an is not 100% Arabic. It contains foreign words borrowed from Ethiopian, Greek, Aramaic, Syriac and other languages.

This verse says that it was given in Arabic to Arabs so they could understand it clearly. Was this because they couldn't read the Tawrat written in Hebrew and the Injil written in Greek? But what about non-

Arabs? How could they understand the Qur'an? Must the entire human race learn Arabic fluently? Still, even if everyone learned Arabic, the Qur'an uses an ancient form of Arabic. Which dialect of Arabic should we learn? Today there are at least 30 dialects of Arabic, with even dozens more local ways of talking. When the 7th century Arabs heard Muhammad recite the Qur'an, they understood exactly what he was saying. Would a modern Arab understand Muhammad if he could travel back in time and listen?

Ayat 4 says that the Qur'an was given in Arabic to the people of Mecca and Medina "to make clear to them." No matter how clear the message was to those people, 1400 years later, the clarity is lost. This is why people rely heavily on the *Tafsir*, interpretations, sheiks and Imams.

My Muslim friends say, "That's true, but you Christians have the same problem. The Injil was written in ancient Greek. Don't you rely heavily on interpretations and translations?" Yes and no. The Injil has been translated into more languages than any other book on earth. We believe that every translation, when done accurately according to the original language, can convey Allah's Word to the reader as well as any other language. We also believe Allah's Spirit guides and instructs individuals without having to have interpretations and explanations.[174]

Humanity's True Essence? (Surah 14:34)

At the core, are humans good, bad or neither? "Verily, man is given

---

[174] Injil, 1 John 2:27, "As for you, the anointing you received from him remains in you, and you do not need anyone to teach you. But as his anointing teaches you about all things and as that anointing is real, not counterfeit—just as it has taught you, remain in him." Comparing the different ways of viewing the language of the Qur'an and Bible introduces the concepts of *vernacular absolutization* and *vernacular translation*. Christians believe that no one language is absolute or holy. Allah understands all human and heavenly languages. Therefore the Tawrat, Prophets and Injil can be freely translated. The truth is holy. The mind of Allah is holy.

up to injustice and ingratitude." In Ayat 22 Satan points out human guilt, "then reproach not me, but reproach your own souls." In the Garden of Eden Adam and Hawwa sinned against Allah. Did Allah immediately stop everything and create a new sinless race? No. But what if he had created new humans? With free-will someone sooner or later would have sinned again. Sin spreads from father to son like a genetic disease. Is it any surprise that all people are given up to injustice and ingratitude?

In the attempt to do good works to please Allah, a shadow is always lurking. Selfishness and pride haunt the most sincere worshipper. One can bow in prayer before Allah then stand and violate his neighbor's rights. Ultimately all injustice and ingratitude is rebellion before Allah. Our reproach comes from breaking his laws. "All of us have become like one who is unclean, and all our righteous acts are like filthy rags; we all shrivel up like a leaf, and like the wind our sins sweep us away."[175] Even our fasting before Allah is tainted with sin. "Your fasting ends in quarreling and strife, and in striking each other with wicked fists. You cannot fast as you do today and expect your voice to be heard on high."[176]

Surely not I? But am I not a member of humanity? Are not my first parents Adam and Hawwa? Along with them have I not been cast out of Paradise?

If this is true, how can anyone ever do more good than evil? In the Great Scale on the Day of Judgment, even my best efforts will be found wanting. The shadow of sin is cast long over the clock of time. The clock is ticking. Time is running out. Still my best efforts are found wanting.

---

[175] Prophets, Yeshaya 64:6

[176] Prophets, Yeshaya 58:4

Chapter 15

Surah 15: Al Hijrah

Allah Protects His Message (Surah 15:9)

Our pace is speeding up with shorter Surahs. This Ayat plainly states that Allah will protect his message. "We have, without doubt, sent down the message; and we will assuredly guard it." No one can corrupt this message (*Zhikra*). The word "message" does not only refer to the Qur'an. It also refers to the Tawrat, Prophets, and Injil.[177]

---

[177] Surah 16:43, "And before thee We sent none but men, to whom We granted inspiration: If ye realise this not, ask of those who possess THE MESSAGE (Zhikri)."

Surah 21:7, "Before thee, also, the messengers We sent were but men, to whom We granted inspiration: if ye know this not, ask of those who possess THE MESSAGE (Zhikri)."

Surah 21:48, "In the past We granted to Moses and Aaron the Criterion (al-Furqana) (for judgment), And a Light and a Message (Zikra) for those who would do right."

Let's be very careful. Allah promises to guard the Word given to Musa and Davud and Isa al-Masih, who is himself the Kalimatullah, the Good News from Heaven. How can man corrupt what Allah guards?

Attacking the Qur'an (Surah 15:91)

Rampant sexual sin and abuse brought Allah's judgment upon the people of Sodom and Gomorrah. Only some of Lut's family escaped. This suggests that judgment could still come upon a nation if it rejects the message of Allah.

The words of Ayat 91 caught my attention. Many Muslim friends tell me that Allah will protect the Qur'an from corruption. But it doesn't mean people couldn't attack the Qur'an with evil motives. This Ayat speaks of certain unbelievers, "as have made Qur'an into shreds." Did they physically shred the Qur'an into pieces? Did they take Ayat out of their context and try to give a new interpretation? Did they make up lies and falsehoods about Muhammad's words? It doesn't say. But reading this Ayat Christians could say that if unbelievers can shred the Qur'an without corrupting it, then they can also shred the Earlier Books without corrupting them.

Surah 21:105, "Before this, We wrote in the Psalms, after THE REMINDER (Zhikri): `My servants, the righteous, shall inherit the earth.'"

Surah 40:53-54, "We did aforetime give Moses the Guidance, and We gave the Book in inheritance to the Children of Israel - A Guide and A REMINDER (Zhikraa) to men of understanding."

Chapter 16

Surah 16: Al Nahl (The Bees)

Created In the Image of Allah? (Surah 16:17)

Much controversy surrounds the story of human origins. The Theory of Evolution says that humans and apes evolved from a common ancestor. It says that if we could go back far enough in time we would see that all animals have a common ancestor that looks like an ugly worm…with a very large mouth.

Many Surah speak about the origin of humans.

> Created man, out of a (mere) clot of congealed blood (96:2).

> We created man from sounding clay, from mud moulded into shape, (15:26).

> The similitude of Jesus before Allah is as that of Adam; He created him from dust, then said to him: "Be". And he was, (3:59).

> But does not man call to mind that We created him

before out of nothing? (19:67, also 52:35).

He has created man from a sperm-drop; and behold this same (man) becomes an open disputer! (16:4)

From these Ayat we can't tell precisely what method Allah used to create humans. Was it from mud, from nothing, a blood clot or something else?

In any case, if we turn in the Tawrat to the very beginning we can read the creation story. Firstly, it says, "In the beginning Allah created the heaven and the earth." Then working through the next six days of creation week, Allah creates the sun and stars, ocean and land, birds, fish and all sorts of animals. As his crowning creation, Allah makes humans.

So God created mankind in his own image, in the image of God he created them; male and female he created them. [178]

What does it mean Allah created humans in his image? Only humans have this distinction. Not cows or horses. Not cats or monkeys.

Surah 16:17 actually gives insight to this question. It asks, "Is then He Who creates like one that creates not?" In other words, isn't Allah a creative Person? All we have to do is look around at the forests and flowers, stars and rivers to realize that Allah must be wonderfully creative. He is creative by nature. He holds the power to create.

Now let's consider humans. It is true that some animals build things. Beavers build dams on rivers and birds build nests in mountain cliffs. They do what Allah put into their instinct. Humans however are amazingly creative. It is true that only Allah can create physical matter out of nothing. But created in Allah's image, humans also can create.

---

[178] Tawrat, Genesis 1:27

The pyramids of Egypt still stand in their awesome power after thousands of years. The music of China lifts human emotions on unseen wings of beauty. Perhaps greatest of all, a husband and wife bring their love together and create a new creative baby boy or girl.[179] Creativity comes from the image of Allah.

All humans are created in Allah's image, but when Adam and Hawwa sinned, the image was horribly distorted. Perfect love became lust. Courage became brutality. Compassion became oppression. Worship became idolatry and self-pride. Justice became murder and war. Sin infected everything. Beauty fell into ugliness and scorn.

Though badly marred, every human still carries the image of Allah. Capable of great inventions and accomplishments, yet continuously pulled downward into pure selfishness, all humans need repair. Or better yet, all humans need a spiritual re-birth. A fresh start. A new image.

> All humans are created in Allah's image, but when Adam and Hawwa sinned, the image was horribly distorted.

The Final Resurrection (Surah 16:38)

Most people have experienced the pain of watching a loved one die. Everyone dies eventually. When the brain, breathing and heart cease their movements, the body quickly grows cold and stiff, destined for decomposition.

Modern scientists say the particles of the body can't possibly reunite and resurrect. For thousands of years natural-minded people have agreed. Surah 16:38 says, "They swear their strongest oaths by Allah, that Allah will not raise up those who die: nay, but it is a promise on

---

[179] Of course all creatures can make babies, but only humans can choose to marry and procreate and then choose how they will raise their children.

him in truth: but most among mankind realize it not." During Isa's time some of the Jewish leaders and Greeks also denied the hope of a resurrection. People demanded, "It's nonsense. Where's the proof?"

No doctor or machine can raise the dead. From a human point of view, resurrection is hopeless. Is there proof? If there is no resurrection from the dead, why not just "eat and drink, for tomorrow we die?"[180]

Allah has not only given his word that resurrection is possible. He has given the ultimate sign. The resurrection of Isa al-Masih on the third day according to ancient prophecies convincingly shows that resurrection from the dead is Allah's will and his promise.

Some may wonder, "What will the final resurrection be like?" Paul explains,

> So will it be with the resurrection of the dead. The body that is sown is perishable, it is raised imperishable; it is sown in dishonor, it is raised in glory; it is sown in weakness, it is raised in power; it is sown a natural body, it is raised a spiritual body. If there is a natural body, there is also a spiritual body.[181]

Like a grain of wheat, the dead body is buried in the soil. At just the right time, it breaks through the surface with new life. The glory of the mature wheat is far greater than the seed. With new fruit and life it grows into the full sunshine. So was the resurrection body of Isa and so shall his followers rise again.

---

[180] Injil, 1 Corinthians 15:32

[181] Injil, 1 Corinthians 15:42-44

Ask a Christian (Surah 16:43)

Should a Muslim ever have need to ask a Christian to explain the Injil?

> And before thee also the messengers We sent were but
> men, to whom We granted inspiration: if ye realize this not,
> ask of those who possess the Message.

Wait! Should a Muslim come to a Christian and ask, "Can you tell us more about Musa, Davud and the other messengers?" The only excuse anyone can give is that the Injil has been changed. But that can't be true. The Injil we have in the 21st century is the same Injil Christians had in the 7th century and in the 1st century. It hasn't changed.

Still, doesn't this verse say that the messengers were "but men?" Doesn't that mean the Christians are wrong about Isa? How can Christians be trusted?

Did we forget what we read about Isa? Only Isa is al-Masih, a prophet and much more, born of a virgin as the new Adam, Kalimatullah, *Emmanuel* which means *Allah with us*. We can talk about Musa and Davud and Yunus as mere men. But we can't honestly include Isa al-Masih as one of them. Isa is more than a messenger. If this Ayat considers Isa only another messenger, I must respectfully disagree. But in addition to the Injil, the Qur'an recognizes that Isa was unique among all people in his work and identify.

For thirty years I have talked with my Muslim friends about the Qur'an and the Injil. Has any Muslim friend ever read Surah 16:43 and asked me to explain the Injil? It makes me sad to say never. Strangely, most of my Muslim friends have never read every Ayat in the Qur'an.

Perhaps a few have read Surah 16:43, but if they are tempted to ask my help, they become afraid. "What will other Muslims say about me?" they think. "Isn't the Injil corrupted? What if Allah punishes me?"

Why would Allah punish someone for simply doing what 16:43 says?

It clearly says, "Ask." It doesn't say dispute. It doesn't say ignore. It doesn't say condemn.

This sounds risky. Maybe Christians want to trick people. Can they be trusted to tell the truth? Aren't they ignorant of the Qur'an? Perhaps some are. But that's why I am reading Ayat by Ayat through the Qur'an: to be fair, to have correct information, to speak truthfully.[182]

Take Not Two Gods (Surah 16:51)

I have said this before, but it is worth saying again. Ayat 51, "Allah has said: take not two gods." The Tawrat, Prophets and Injil *do not* support the polytheists (*mushrikun*). The first and greatest command is to love Allah with all our heart, mind and strength. How can we give 100% of ourselves to the One True Allah and have anything left to give to another god?

No One Good (Surah 16:61)

Ayat 61 agrees with the Injil that no one is good. "If Allah were to punish men for their wrong doing, he would not leave, on the (earth), a single living creature." The diagnosis of the human heart is that something is wrong. Everyone deserves punishment. Standing at this intersection in the pathways of the Injil and Qur'an, I notice they answer the problem of evil differently. The Injil takes me toward the Heavenly gift of forgiveness lovingly offered in al-Masih. The Qur'an takes me toward a divine scale that weighs my good and bad deeds. But Ayat 61 tells us that everyone is equally deserving of punishment! The effort to build a house of righteousness is utterly swept away by a tsunami of sin. Who will deliver us from this certain judgment?

Slavery (Surah 16:71-76)

---

[182] This is also why I am including information from the Tawrat, Prophets and Injil. Surah 16:43 tells Muslims to ask Christians for help.

Western countries have outlawed human slavery. In the 1860s the United States fought a horrendous civil war ending slavery there and liberating millions of African-Americans.

Ayat 75-76 enters the discussion about human equality. It says a slave is not equal to his generous and noble master and a handicapped and powerless man is not equal to the strong. The Qur'an asks, "Is such a man equal with one who commands justice, and is on a straight way?"

Qur'anic Sharia is unlike Western secular legal systems. While Western secular laws recognize equality between people of different races, religions and all kinds of backgrounds, classic Sharia does not. At times under Sharia non-Muslims have had to live as dhimmis and some classes of people worked as slaves. In the 21st century slavery is still practiced in various places based on Ayat like these. Just as Muslims continue to debate whether military jihad still applies in the modern world, they also discuss the practice of slavery.

Each People Their Own Witness (Surah 16:89)

We saw in Surah 14:4 that Muhammad went to Arabs who spoke Arabic. Now Ayat 89 says,

> One day we shall raise from all peoples a witness against them, from amongst themselves: and we shall bring thee as a witness against these; and we have sent down to thee the book explaining all things...

Years ago I sat with my friend drinking tea under the shade of a grape vine. He said, "Did you know that Allah sent Musa and Isa to the Jews? And that he sent every nation their own prophet?"

"No," I replied, "I hadn't heard that before." It was hard for me to imagine for example what prophets went to the Vikings or the Native American tribes.

The Qur'an says Muhammad was sent to the Arabs. If every different tribe and people group has had a witness, what is the purpose of taking them Muhammad's message in the Arabic language, which they don't understand? Didn't they already have a witness sent in their own language?

Furthermore, Ayat 89 clearly says that Allah sent Muhammad as a witness against the Arabs. In this Ayat at least, it does not claim that he is a witness to all peoples.

A Change in Mind (Surah 16:106-107)

The Qur'an permits a Muslim to call himself an unbeliever to protect himself, as long as he still truly believes in his heart. However, if a person truly changes his mind and heart and leaves Islam, he or she is warned of a severe penalty.

> Anyone who, after accepting Faith in Allah, utters unbelief, except under compulsion, his heart remaining firm in Faith, but such as open their breast to unbelief, on them is wrath from Allah, and theirs will be a dreadful penalty.

In 1844 Sultan Abdülmejid 1ˢᵗ ended the law of apostasy in the Turkish Osman Empire, allowing Muslims to leave Islam without penalty of execution. His edict was not always obeyed. Classical Sharia requires that apostates be executed.

Why would a Muslim leave Islam? Ayat 107 says that "they love the life of this world better than the Hereafter." We have seen how the Qur'an accuses some Muslims of hypocrisy when they preferred the comfort of their homes and wealth to marching out to wage war in the way of Allah. Living for Islam in the 7ᵗʰ century could be dangerous.

Do some Muslims leave Islam for reasons other than to avoid injury or death in battle? I have a friend who left Islam because he became convinced that there is no Creator. He thinks the universe created itself. He calls himself a scientific atheist. Other people I know changed their minds because they studied and chose to believe other ideas.

If a modern Muslim risks rejection from family and friends, and in some places execution for apostasy, how does his or her life improve by leaving Islam? Unless a war breaks out where Muslims are called to face dire peril in the cause of Allah, the easiest thing would be to leave everything the same.

Spread Islam (Surah 16:125)

In an old stone courtyard our small group of friends talked late into the evening about faith in Allah. One said, "Missionary work is wrong in my opinion. Islam has no missionary work."

"Strange," I replied, "because I've met Muslims who, for example, work very hard in Europe and Africa trying to persuade non-Muslims to embrace Islam."

Perhaps our friend never read Ayat 125,

> Invite to the way of thy Lord with wisdom and beautiful preaching; and argue with them in ways that are best and Most Gracious: for thy Lord knoweth best, who have strayed from his path, and who receive guidance.

Muslims who take this Ayat seriously give of their time and money spreading Islam around the world. Devout Muslims have set up offices and mosques in nearly every country of the earth. They write books, enter public debates and spread their ideas on television, radio and the internet. They are Muslim missionaries.

"No, that's incorrect," my friends sometimes reply. "A *missionary* is someone who uses compulsion to make people change their religion. Muslims only speak the truth to invite unbelievers to the way of Allah." Do Christian missionaries use money, politics and brain-washing to make converts? Do they have a dark purpose to impose their will on helpless people? Rumors say they put $100 bills in the Injil—I suppose with inflation that's gone up to $1000—hoping to steal someone from the Straight Way. Other times friends say, "I don't think Muslims should try to actively spread their faith. Religion is a private matter."

I see two mistakes here. First, any Christian who tried to use money or politics to change someone's religion is a phony. A true Christian believes in authenticity. Choosing the truth isn't like choosing a football team. For example, if I wanted more people to come watch my favorite football team play a match, I might offer free tickets just so it looks like there are more fans. What do I care if they really like my team or not? But calling people to faith in Allah is a matter of true love. You can't buy true love.

Second, anyone who thinks Muslims should keep Islam private has failed to read Ayat 125. It is not talking about inviting fellow Muslims to Jumu'ah prayers at the mosque. It is talking about trying to persuade unbelievers to embrace Islam. This is not private but public. In the world of ideas a thousand voices call out each day, claiming to have the best or the only true idea.

Chapter 17

Surah 17: Al Isra' (The Night Journey)
or Bani Isra'il (The Children of Israel)

Visit to Kudus (Surah 17:1)

History is important. Knowing history makes us wise. We know from history that al-Aqsa Mosque (الْمَسْجِدْأَقْصَى) was constructed on the foundation of Suleiman's temple sometime between 679-690 CE. The Masjid al-Haram (الْمَسْجِدِ الْحَرَام) in Mecca was constructed at the Ka'aba about 690 CE. We also know that Muhammad lived between 570-632 CE. Knowing these things makes Surah 17:1 puzzling. It says,

> Glory to, who did take his servant for a journey by night from the sacred Mosque to the farthest Mosque, whose precincts we did bless, in order that we might show him some of our Signs: for he is the one who heareth and seeth.

The Night Visit (*Miraj*) is only mentioned in one Ayat of the Qur'an. There are no details, no names, no dates. This Ayat doesn't even say specifically what servant traveled or what cities he visited? It gives no explanation why the servant traveled to the farthest mosque or how he made the journey.

It is generally believed that the servant was Muhammad, the sacred mosque was the Masjid al-Haram and the farthest mosque was al-Aqsa. Without knowing history, someone might think this is not puzzling. People just assume that Muhammad visited the buildings still standing today. But history shows that both the Mecca and Kudus mosques were built about 60 years after Muhammad died.

Some have argued that the word mosque (الْمَسْجِدِ) refers only to a special piece of ground. I am not qualified to say. But since the mosques standing today in Mecca and Kudus were built 60 years after Muhammad died, this Ayat cannot refer to those buildings. Muhammad could not have visited al-Aqsa in Kudus because it did not exist yet.

Surah 17:1 leaves us with only a few words and more questions. Written many years after Muhammad, the Hadith expand on this topic. Sahih al-Bukhari writes that Muhammad saw with his own eyes the *Bait-ul-Maqdis* (al Aqsa in Kudus).[183] But this wasn't physically possible because Muhammad had been dead 60 years when his followers started constructing al Aqsa.

As an Isa follower, I wonder about the purpose of the journey. I'm interested to see how Islam started, consolidated power and established centers in Medina, Mecca and Kudus. I'm interested to learn how Muslims extended the borders of Islam beyond Arabia and into the heartland of the children of Ibrahim, conquering Kudus and building the al Aqsa mosque just 60 years after Muhammad's death.

No ancient inscriptions have been found in the al Aqsa mosque referring to the Night Visit (miraj). But pointing to Surah 17:1, later traditions developed the idea that Kudus was a place of special importance to Muslims. It became a symbol of Islamic dominance over Judaism and Christianity, proof that Islam had superseded the

---

[183] Sahih al-Bukhari, Volume 5, Book 58, Number 228 and Volume 6, Book 60, Number 233

earlier prophetic religions. Muslims reasoned that if Muhammad had visited Kudus, they had a responsibility to guard it for Islam. People believed the al Aqsa mosque and the Dome on the Rock covering the former Jewish Temple Mount guaranteed that Jews would never again attempt to rise from the ashes and try to reassert themselves by building a new Jewish Temple. For many Al Aqsa mosque is like a huge stone seal permanently stamped onto the city of Kudus, insuring that Islam will always have the highest place over unbelievers.[184]

---

[184] 9:29 "Fight those who believe not in Allah nor the Last Day, nor hold that forbidden which hath been forbidden by Allah and His Messenger, nor acknowledge the Religion of truth, from among the People of the Book, until they pay the Jizyah with willing submission, and feel themselves subdued." In 846 an Arab expeditionary force attacked the Roman Catholic head city of Rome. They plundered treasures and were eventually repelled. In 1453 the army of Fatih Sultan Mehmet prevailed over the walls of Istanbul, conquering the seat of the Eastern Orthodox Church and turning the Hagia Sofia Cathedral into a mosque.

Chapter 18

Surah 18: Al Kahf (The Cave)

The Cave Sleepers (Surah 18:9-26)

Leaving Ephesus one morning on a long taxi ride, I listened to my driver tell the story of the Seven Sleepers. On the edge of the ancient city ruins, tourists can find a cave or two where some young men allegedly took a miraculous nap for hundreds of years. The story says they awoke to a great shock when they saw how much the world had changed since they first fell asleep.

The first records of the story come from the 5th and 6th centuries written by the scholars Yakup of Saruq, Theodosius and Dionysius of Tell Mahra in a Syriac work. Many ordinary people in the Mediterranean region knew the story.

Surah 19 gives few details about the Seven Sleepers. It does not say the cave was near Ephesus or any other known city. It does not say when it happened and does not name any rulers or kings. Muhammad says he doesn't know how many men took the long nap: were there three with a dog, four and the dog, five, six and a dog, or seven and the dog?

This makes me curious. Why didn't Allah reveal in the Qur'an how many sleepers there were, since he would have known? The same problem occurs with the number of years they slept. Was it 300 years or 200 hundred or something else? Ayat 26 says, "Allah knows best how long they stayed: with him is the secrets of the heavens and the earth."

As a student of history and the Earlier Books, I always evaluate the past with certain questions. One, did Isa prophecy this would happen? For example, he prophesied that the Kudus Temple would be destroyed and it was. Many historical events have occurred that Isa did not specifically predict, but I pay special attention to the ones he did predict would happen. Did Isa predict anything like the Seven Sleepers? Not that I can find.

Two, is the story supported by historical evidence? Not really. There is a cave in Ephesus with tombs, but there are no eyewitnesses to anyone sleeping for hundreds of years. It sounds like folklore instead of fact.

Three, if I discover that a sacred story is not historical, does anything change in my beliefs about Allah's loving relationship with his people? For example, how would my relationship with Allah change if I discovered that the story of the parting of the Red Sea never really happened? It would shake my confidence in Allah's Word. While I agree with Surah 18 that Allah does miracles and knows everything, historical or not, the Seven Sleepers story does not personally impact my relationship with the Lord.

"None can Change His Words" (Surah 18:27)

We have come a long way in the Qur'an. No where have we seen evidence that the Tawrat, Prophets and Injil have been corrupted. We have seen the opposite. Once again we read in Ayat 27, "none can change His words." How many times does this need to be repeated until we understand?

Earning Allah's Favor (Surah 18:46-53)

Walking the Qur'an pathway brings me to another critical juncture. This passage says that good works contribute to reaching Heaven. Allah has a book where he records every deed, apparently both good and evil. Ayat 46,

> good deeds, are best in the sight of thy Lord, as rewards, and best as (the foundation for) hopes.

One day a Muslim friend asked me, "Doesn't your religion promise Heaven even to bad people, just as long as they confess their sins to a priest? You don't have to do good deeds. You just confess and then go out and sin all you want? In Islam we must do good works if we hope to reach Paradise."

Good question.

Imagine a man with a horse and a wagon. Wanting to take home a load of flour, he rolls the wagon in front of the horse and starts yelling at it. He wants the wagon to pull the horse! The wagon can't pull anything, it needs the horse to pull it.

This is what Isa meant when he said, "I am the vine; you are the branches. If you remain in me and I in you, you will bear much fruit; apart from me you can do nothing."[185]

Trying to pull a horse with a wagon is like trying to do good works to please Allah.

Why? Because without a right relationship with Allah, our works are powerless to please him. A wagon can't pull a horse because it has no power. Left alone, the wagon only sits motionless. Alone in our brokenness and sinfulness, even our best works can't please Allah.

The Injil teaches that we must first trust in Allah to regenerate us and then we can produce truly good works in His power. This is putting

---

[185] Injil, John 15:5

the horse before the cart.

Therefore, good works are the fruit of Allah's favor upon us, not the cause of it. The Injil says, "For it is by grace you have been saved, through faith—and this is not from yourselves, it is the gift of God..."[186]

"So you don't believe in good works, after all!" my friend replied.

"Please don't miss the point," I said. "We absolutely believe in good works. If anyone claims to be a new person in al-Masih but doesn't produce good works, he is a liar. Isa said that good trees bear good fruit and bad trees bear bad fruit. Anyone who desires more and more sinful behavior still has a dead heart, no matter how many times they confess their sins."[187]

Was Iblis an Angel or a Jinn? (Surah 18:50)

Iblis' identity is a mystery. Surah 2:34 includes Iblis among the angels. He is condemned for not bowing before Adam along with the angels. Now we read that he was a Jinn.

> Behold we said to the angels, bow down to Adam they bowed down except Iblis. He was one of the Jinn, and he broke the command of his Lord.

Allah commanded the angels to bow. If Allah wanted the Jinn to bow too, why were they not included? If angels and jinn are the same thing, why would they have different names? They have other differences too. One Muslim writes, "Angels are created from light while Jinns are created from fire...all the angels are believers who are infallible and they only ever enjoin others to do good. Among the Jinns, there are

---

[186] Injil, Ephesians 2:8

[187] Injil, Matthew 7:7

Muslims and disbelievers, as well as those who enjoin good and those who enjoin evil… Angels do not have desires, unlike Jinns who have desires just like humans."[188]

If I may be honest, I admit it's hard for me to envision any Heavenly creature bowing before Adam. He was a mere man, creature of dust, a would-be sinner, earthly. Perhaps Adam would bow in respect before an angel. But no one is worthy of adoration except Allah alone. All of creation will fall before him alone and declare, "You are worthy, our Lord and God, to receive glory and honor and power, for you created all things, and by your will they were created and have their being."[189]

Zul Qarnain, Lord of Two Horns (Surah 18:83-99)

We come to another mysterious identity. Many Muslims have thought that Zul Qarnain was Alexander the Great, the Greek warrior who conquered a huge swath of Asia. But Surah 18 describes this mysterious person as a servant of Allah. How could this be Alexander? History shows that he practiced homosexuality and idolatry. Others have suggested this Ayat refers to Cyrus the Great, the Persian ruler who showed favor to the children of Ibrahim. But he practiced Zoroastrianism even though he was friendly to the monotheist Jews. Anyone who suggests that Alexander or Cyrus were Muslims needs to explain how a polytheist (mushrik) can also be a Muslim.

Where Does the Sun Set? (Surah 18:86)

"Did you know that Jacque Cousteau become a Muslim? His travels in the oceans convinced him the Qur'an is true." My friend felt happy

---

[188] "The difference between angels, Jinns and devils", Islamweb, http://www.islamweb.net/emainpage/index.php?Id=16265&Option=FatwaId&page=showfatwa, accessed February 2018.

[189] Injil, Revelation 4:11

to share the story of the famous marine scientist. I listened with interest.

Many friends believe the Qur'an contains scientific facts that Muhammad could have known only by divine revelation. If the Qur'an does have scientific facts miraculously revealed, they would make a strong case for Islam. I researched Cousteau and found this official letter from his offices in France.

> Paris, November 2, 1991
>
> Sir,
>
> We have received your letter and we thank you for your interest in our activities.
>
> We state precisely to you that Commander Cousteau has not become a Muslim and that this rumor passes around without foundation.
>
> Very cordially,
>
> Didier CERCEAU
>
> Chargé de mission[190]

I don't know if Cousteau ever read the Qur'an. He certainly knew a lot about the ocean. At death his family buried him in a Christian cemetery in France. There is no evidence he became a Muslim.

Still, it is fair to ask, does the Qur'an miraculously reveal scientific facts?

---

[190] "Jacques Cousteau (Conversion to Islam)", WikiIslam, http://wikiislam.net/wiki/Jacques_Cousteau_ (Conversion_to_Islam), accessed February 2018.

I studied science in college, getting my first degree in microbiology. My training prepared me in the methods of observation and testing. Furthermore, the Injil teaches me to "test everything."[191] Science is only as successful as human intellect. Human minds are not perfect, but scientists like Pasteur and Rontgen have made great discoveries that vastly improve health and life. We know so much more about the earth and sea, sun and stars in the 21st century than people knew a thousand years ago.

Human curiosity is innate. Humans explore and discover regardless of the obstacles they may face. Polynesians in small canoes sailed into the Pacific Ocean with no map or compass. Yet they found the islands of Hawaii and started a new kingdom there. It was natural for Arabs to wonder about the natural order. For example, they looked at the sun and asked, "What is it and where does it go every night?"

Surah 18:86 says that when Zul Qarnain "reached the setting of the sun, he found it set in a spring of murky water: near it he found a people." Sunan Abu Davud 3991 records,

> Abu Dharr said: I was sitting behind the Apostle of Allah who was riding a donkey while the sun was setting. He asked: Do you know where this sets? I replied: Allah and his Apostle know best. He said: It sets in a spring of warm water.

Perhaps Ayat 86 is an allegory. It is hard to know the original intent. But in the 21st century we know that the sun does not set in water. This is not a scientific statement. We can read many interesting stories and illustrations about Allah in the Tawrat, Prophets, Injil and Qur'an, but they do not give technical scientific information.

What do I mean? Imagine if the Qur'an said, "Zul Qarnain looked in the sky and realized the sun is a huge exploding ball of nuclear energy

---

[191] Injil, 1 Thessalonians 5:21

vastly bigger than the earth and 330,000 times farther away from it than Medina is from Mecca?" In the 6th century it would have been practically impossible for Muhammad to have known the sun's distance from the earth or known that it is a colossal burning ball of nuclear energy. The Tawrat, Prophets, Injil and Qur'an don't talk like that. They don't tell us how to build an airplane or cure cancer. They don't explain how the moon orbits the earth and the earth orbits the sun. The Qur'an contains many interesting observations about nature, but if someone wants to prove it came from Allah, he or she will want to find ways other than looking for miraculously revealed scientific facts.

Chapter 19

Surah 19: Miriam

The Prophet Yahiya (Surah 19:1-15)

Many stories show that Allah likes giving people babies, especially to parents who think they can't have any. He gave Ibrahim and Sara baby Isak when they were long past the ripe age. He gave Miriam baby Isa without the help of a human father. Zakary and Elisabeth also got a special gift from Allah when he gave them Yahiya in their old age.

Zakary (Zacharias) was a Hebrew priest living in the days of King Herod of Judea. His wife Elisabeth came from the family of Harun (Aaron), who had lived a thousand years earlier. One day while worshipping in the Temple of Kudus, Zakary met an angel. The Lord promised to give them a son, but Zakary was skeptical. To prove his word and discipline Zakary, the Lord took away his speech for several months. When Yahiya was born his parents took him to the Temple for circumcision. As the family discussed what name to choose, Zakary wrote the name Yahiya on a tablet and immediately his voice returned.

Yahiya was set apart for a very special purpose. He didn't eat or drink anything alcoholic, lived in the wilderness and wore rough camel skins. As a young man he started baptizing people in the Jordan River as a sign of new spiritual life. Large crowds came to him, stirring deep jealousy in the Jewish religious leaders.

Yahiya was a herald. "A voice of one calling in the wilderness, 'Prepare the way for the Lord, make straight paths for him.'"[192] Like a viceroy going before the sultan, Yahiya went before the coming Masih, preparing his way.

One warm day the crowds gathered next to the Jordan River, eager to hear Yahiya's words and let him immerse them in the water. It was an ordinary day for Yahiya, until an extraordinary person stepped out of the crowd. Yahiya must have trembled when he looked at the young, bearded man standing before him. "I'm not even worthy to untie his sandals," he thought.

He looked at Isa and said, "You should be baptizing me."

In humility Isa replied "Let it be, to fulfill all righteousness."

Obediently, Yahiya took Isa into the river and dipped him under the cold, dark waters.

Suddenly an opening appeared in the sky and a dove fluttered down and landed on Isa. They heard the voice of Allah. "This is my Son, whom I love; with him I am well pleased."[193]

What happened there? Two essential things. Confirmation and commendation. The children of Ibrahim had been waiting for thousands of years for their Masih. They needed a way to recognize him from the crowd. He looked like any other bearded carpenter from Galilee. Yahiya confirmed that Isa was al-Masih. Yahiya came to

---

[192] Injil, Luke 3:4

[193] Injil, Matthew 3; Injil, Luke 3

announce, "Isa is the One."

Muslim friends often stop me here. "Not again, please. Why do we keep hearing the word *son?* The Injil won't let it go. Why can't Christians see how they are obviously worshipping three gods?"

Let's consider a new approach. The ancient scholar Augustine wrote, "And the Holy Spirit, according to the Holy Scriptures, is neither of the Father alone, nor of the Son alone, but of both; and so intimates to us a mutual love, wherewith the Father and the Son reciprocally love one another."[194]

Here is what *son* does NOT mean. It does not mean Allah has a physical body and took Miriam (or anyone) as his wife. It does not mean that Isa is a second god associated with Allah. It does not mean that Isa's self-essence was created long ago. What it does mean is that Allah, from his own self-essence, clothed himself in the human Isa al-Masih. He lived among us with the purpose of making it possible to be forgiven through his sacrifice on the cross.

We saw earlier that the Tawrat often calls Allah merciful (Rahman) and compassionate (Rahim). History shows that long before Muhammad was born, ancient Syriac Christians used the title *Al Rahmana* for Isa.[195] This is a full vision of Allah. Mercy and compassion are not simply feelings or attitudes. The most merciful thing Allah could do was come to the earth and provide the perfect, holy sacrifice for our sins. His

---

[194] Augustine, *On the Trinity* XV.17.2

[195] "Meaning of AR RAHMAN", The Qur'an and Its Message, "That al-Raḥmān should have been the name of a single God in central and southern Arabia is in no way incompatible with the fact that, when adopted by Islam, it assumes a grammatical form of a word derived from the root RḤM."

http://Qur'ansmessage.com/forum/index.php?topic=1320.0, accessed February 2018.

mercy and compassion are the fruits of his divine love.

Isa's Death (Surah 19:33)

"Just a moment," I said to my neighbor, "you keep showing me Surah 4:156 to prove that Isa did not die. I don't think it says that Isa did not die, but that the Jews did not kill him. Are there any verses in the Qur'an that say Isa did not die?"

I waited, but my friend could not answer. There are none.

In fact, we keep discovering more verses that say Isa died. For example, Ayat 33-34 says,

> So peace is on me The day I was born, the day that I die, and the day that I shall be raised up to life! Such Jesus the son of Mary.

What?! Not only does it say he would die, but it precisely matches Surah 3:55 in the order of events. Isa lived, died and was raised from the dead. How can this not be fascinating to anyone who knows the Injil?

Chapter 20

Surah 20: Ta Ha

Musa and the Burning Bush (Surah 20)

Surah 20 sparks many intriguing considerations. I'll focus on some of the highlights.

First, I notice that Musa personally heard the voice of Allah. The story goes like this.[196] Musa saw a fire far away on a mountain. Curious, he climbed closer. Out of a strangely burning tree, Allah himself spoke audibly to Musa, telling him to remove his sandals because the ground was holy. Allah then instructed Musa to return to Egypt and join his brother Harun to tell the Pharaoh to release the children of Ibrahim from captivity. Musa went back to Egypt, the Pharaoh did not obey Allah, a number of plagues fell on Egypt, he finally freed the slaves and then Allah drowned the Egyptian

> Love stories always include speaking. This love story involves divine communication.

---

[196] See Tawrat, Exodus 3 for more details.

army in the Red Sea. After escaping the Egyptians through the Red Sea, some of the Hebrews crafted and worshipped a golden calf while Musa received the Ten Commandments on the mountain. When Musa returned, Allah's wrath fell on the idolaters and yet some of Musa's faithful people were saved.

Ayat 11-12 say, "But when he came to the fire, a voice was heard: O Musa! Verily I am thy Lord!" Notice, Allah did not speak through an angel to Musa.

History is the Grand Story of the Lord's Love. It starts in the Garden of Eden with Adam and Hawwa and then develops with Ibrahim, Musa, Shammil, and King Davud. In the Injil the story leads us across the threshold into the most holy place with Isa al-Masih. This Love Story always involves divine communication. Allah's Word (or Voice) isn't just *with* him, he *is* the Kalimatullah, Allah's essence.

Why is direct communication so important? Someone has said that communication is the life-blood of any relationship. Loving husbands and wives spend time talking and listening, sharing their hearts and not just their bodies. Love makes parents sit down and talk with their children and it makes good friends take time to communicate about their lives.

Is it impossible for Allah to speak directly with his people? Why not? He spoke to Adam and Hawwa, like a father speaks with his children. He spoke to Musa, like friends talking together.

When Isa, the Word of Allah, came, he told his disciples that they were no longer his servants, but friends. He said that no greater love has anyone than freely giving his life for his friends.[197] Allah's Grand Love Story shows that the first perfect friendship was ruined by disobedience in the Garden but Allah gradually rebuilt the bridge of

---

[197] Injil, John 15:13

love. Isa was the cornerstone.

Imagine a man in love with a woman living on the other side of the ocean. First he sends her hand-written letters. Then he talks with her over the telephone. Finally he boards an airplane and travels to her side. When they meet face to face their joy is complete.

For this reason, in some Muslim societies people have come to think of Allah in a new way and call themselves Lovers of Allah (عشاق الله). "Perfect love casts out all fear."[198] Meeting Allah through al-Masih brings people back to the place of no shame, like Adam enjoyed before he sinned. Without shame, without guilt, without fear of any punishment, we can relate to Allah with love pouring down continuously from the mountains of Heaven like a mighty waterfall.

Adam's Shame (Surah 20:115-123)

Naked before Allah in thought and body, Adam vainly attempted to hide his shame. He and Hawwa knit fig leaves together for a covering. Everyone shares their shame. Most humans still cover their bodies with robes and scarves, dresses, pants or sometimes grass and gourds. Public nakedness is a sign of indifference to Allah.

We read in the Tawrat that Allah did not accept the covering of leaves. Instead, he gave Adam and Hawwa new coverings. Allah himself sacrificed animals and covered Adam and Hawwa with the skins. Allah teaches us that our good works are insufficient and defective. The only covering for our inner shame is the sacrifice he provides. This is why al-Masih said that he came not to be served but to serve and give his life as a ransom for us.

---

[198] Injil, 1 John 4:18

Chapter 21

Surah 21: Al Anbiya' (The Prophets)

Names of Muhammad (Surah 21:107)

The message of this Surah is simple. Turn from polytheism to belief in one Allah and accept Muhammad.

Ayat 107 brings us to an interesting question. What is the relationship between the names of Muhammad and the Beautiful Names? For example, in this Ayat we read that Muhammad is the *Mercy* (رَحْمَة) from Allah. "We sent thee not, but as a Mercy for all creatures." In Surah 1:1 we read that Allah is *Al Rahman* (الرَّحِيم). Another example is Surah 22:64 and Surah 61:6. Surah 22:64 calls Allah *Hamid* (الْحَمِيدُ). In Surah 61:6 we see Ahmed (أَحْمَدُ) is used for Muhammad.

The book *Dalail-ul-Khairat: Guide of Good Deeds* gives the list of 99 Names of Allah (*Asma Al Husna*) and 201 Names of the Prophet (*Asma An Nabi*). Many of the names have the same root except the names of Allah have the definite article *Al*.

Like all men before him, Muhammad came from a father who came from Adam and Hawwa. We know that Muhammad died as did all other men and he returned to the soil. Though many great leaders have lived in history, we do not glorify them. For example, though Musa met with Allah in the burning bush and received the Ten Commandments, he shared common humanity with everyone in whose veins run the blood of Adam. As someone said, the blood of Adam should make the greatest king lower his head in shame and the lowest beggar lift his in honor.

Surah 3:144 says, "Muhammad is no more than a messenger like the messengers that have already passed away before him; if then he dies or is killed will you turn back upon your heels?" Does this caution people to avoid lifting up prophets too highly?

Chapter 22

Surah 22: Al Hajj (The Pilgrimage)

Arguing from Ignorance (Surah 22:8)

Often my friends freely give me their opinion about Allah, Isa, the Injil and the Qur'an. They have picked up some ideas here and there, but have not personally read every verse of the Tawrat, Prophets, Injil and Qur'an. The Qur'an warns against arguing from ignorance. Ayat 8, "Yet there is among men such a one as disputes about Allah, without knowledge, without guidance, and without a Book of enlightenment." I write this book as my pilgrimage away from ignorance.

Hell (Surah 22:19-22)

The Qur'an gives a consistent and vivid picture of Hell.

> those who deny, for them will be cut out a garment of Fire: over their heads will be poured out boiling water. With it will be scalded what is within their bodies, as well as skins. In addition there will be maces of iron them. Every time they wish to get away therefrom from anguish."

I can't picture anything more hideous. Intense pain wracks the body as boiling water showers down from fire overhead. Anyone who can muster the strength to escape the torment and suffering ripping through their bodies will meet the crushing blows of an iron mace. And it never, ever ends. Endless torment. Eternal pain.

Modern people balk at this belief. It reminds many of a bedtime story about monsters with big teeth waiting outside the house, eager to devour any child who disobeys his parents. "Don't get out of bed after dark," they say, "or the vicious monster with yellow eyes and teeth dripping with blood will pounce on you before you can blink your sleepy eyes. And even worse, if you forget to brush your teeth, he will sneak out from under your bed and chew your legs off at mid-night. Then you will wake up with no teeth and no legs."

Richard Dawkins thinks that teaching a child about Hell is abusive.

> Thank goodness, I have never personally experienced what it is like to believe – really and truly and deeply believe –– in Hell. But I think it can be plausibly argued that such a deeply held belief might cause a child more long-lasting mental trauma than the temporary embarrassment of mild physical abuse.[199]

On the other hand, a wealthy and educated Muslim man told me that people need stories about Hell. He didn't really believe in Allah, but he said that society needs the fear of Hell to keep people in line.[200] He reckoned that the fear of Hell deters criminals and makes people obey

---

[199] "Richard Dawkins and Hell", Conservapedia, http://www.conservapedia.com/Richard_Dawkins_and_Hell, accessed February 2018.

[200] Scott A. McGreal, "Belief in Hell: Does it Benefit or Harm Society?", Psychology *Today*, https://www.psychologytoday.com/blog/unique-everybody-else/201312/belief-in-Hell-does-it-benefit-or-harm-society, accessed February 2018.

the laws. For him, Hell is like the yellow-eyed monster, just a bedtime story to scare children into brushing their teeth.

The Qur'an uses the word Hell (جَهَنَّم) 77 times, fire 172 and burn 41.[201] Many more Ayat talk about judgment and torment without using the word Hell. Paradise (ٱلْجَنَّة) appears 102 times in various forms.[202] The Qur'an hammers into the reader's mind the idea that good Muslims will have eternal pleasures and non-Muslims will have eternal pain.

The concept of Hell did not originate with the Qur'an. Many early prophets and Isa al-Masih warned that the wicked would perish in a dark place separated from Allah. The plagues that fell upon the Pharaoh and his people in Egypt demonstrated the consequence of deliberately turning away from Allah.

The Hebrew word describing the place of darkness is *Sheol* (שְׁאוֹל) and the Injil uses the word *Hades* (ᾅδης). At other times we read how the ancient people of Kudus tossed their trash and even corpses into the deep gorge of Gehenna on the edge of the city. Anyone who heard Isa describe Gehenna could immediately imagine the repulsive smoke and stench.

Compared to the Qur'an, the Injil gives few details about Hell. It says, "Then death and Hades were thrown into the lake of fire. The lake of fire is the second death. Anyone whose name was not found written in the book of life was thrown into the lake of fire."[203] Isa says that those who lived for themselves would pass way into "eternal punishment."[204]

---

[201] Total numbers may differ depending on word form in Arabic.

[202] Tawrat, Zabur and Injil have 54 references to the terminology of something like Hell.

[203] Injil, Revelation 20:14-15

[204] Injil, Matthew 25:46

The idea of Hell deeply troubled one of my best friends. He believed in Allah and loved Masih Isa. We had many conversations about Allah's love and the problem of Hell. Many people share his questions. How can Allah truly be loving and condemn people to eternal punishment?

Here's an example of another man who wrote how he can't imagine living in Heaven at the same time others are suffering in Hell.

> God, allow me to exchange places, please, because, if You're expecting me to be happy floating around in heaven on a cloud singing hymns about your compassion and grace and love all day long, knowing some of my friends and others are suffering in Hell...You're wrong. You're dead wrong. In fact, Your heaven has just become my Hell![205]

Among Muslims there are also many questions about Hell. Is it eternal? Is there an exit from Hell after a period of time? Must all Muslims pass through Hell?[206] Do some Muslims go to Hell and then get out after being punished for small sins? Can Christians, Jews and even idol worshippers eventually get out of Hell? Will Hell be empty some day? The Ahmadiyya sect and others believe that Hell may one day be completely empty when every soul is set free.

Ezekiel the prophet wrote, "'For I take no pleasure in the death of anyone,' declares the Sovereign Lord. 'Repent and live!'"[207] When Isa approached Kudus, he gazed over the city and shed tears. How his

---

[205] Steve McSwain, "Why I Do Not Believe in Hell", Huffpost, https://www.huffingtonpost.com/steve-mcswain/why-i-do-not-believe-in-h_b_7762130.html, accessed February 2018.

[206] Surah 19:71, 72. نَقُّوا (waruda) means "to meet", in this case it speaks about meeting the fires of Hell.

[207] Prophets, Ezekiel 18:32

heart broke for the sinful people![208] Allah sent al-Masih because he loved the human race and did not wish for our destruction.

Allah has revealed that Heaven and Hell are real places. I understand the Injil to say that at the end of time he will judge every human. Some will pass into eternal life in the very presence of Allah. Others will go into eternal Hell.[209]

If Hell is real, doesn't that mean Allah isn't truly loving? If Allah is truly loving, does that mean Hell can't exist? How can Allah be both loving and punish sinful people in Hell? It's as though these two things can't exist at the same time.

Isa gives us a window into this question. Because Allah is loving, he provided a cure for our sin disease. Because he is just, he caused the punishment for sin to fall upon Isa al-Masih on the cross. Those who believe in Isa are justified and saved from Hell. Those who do not accept this free offer of the cure for sin must face the punishment in Hell. Allah is perfectly good, loving and just. Love motivated his offer of forgiveness through the death and resurrection of Isa. Justice requires him to give the proper punishment to sinners who reject the sacrificial Lamb of Allah. Justice also requires him to give eternal life to the one who takes shelter in the blood of the Lamb.

Power to Create (Surah 22:73)

We can say that humans are creative. But only Allah can create something from nothing. Only he can create life. This Ayat says,

> O men! Here is a parable set forth! listen to it! those on

---

[208] Injil, Luke 19:41-44.

[209] Some of my Christian brothers read the Tawrat, Prophets and Injil and conclude that Allah will annihilate rebellious people after the judgment. Though I disagree, I can respectfully listen to them.

whom, besides Allah, ye call, cannot create a fly.

Idols and false gods are powerless. False gods do not create.

This verse immediately calls to mind Surah 5:110, which says,

> And behold! thou makest out of clay, as it were, the figure of a bird, by My leave, and thou breathest into it, and it becometh a bird by My leave.

While false gods cannot create anything, not even a fly, this Surah claims that Isa al-Masih has a relationship with Allah so intimate, Allah breathed through him to create a new bird.

Chapter 23

Surah 23: Al Mu'minun (The Believers)

Creation of Humans (Surah 23:12-14)

The story of Isa's creation of the bird is a good transition to Surah 23. This Surah presents several stages of human creation: clay, semen, blood clot, lump, bones and then flesh. I'm not sure if this is describing only the creation of Adam or every human. In either case, medical science shows that this passage does not describe actual human development in the womb. Perhaps it is meant poetically.

This is one of many times the Qur'an describes the creation of humans. What are these Ayat meant to tell us? They show that humans have humble beginnings. They show that Allah is powerful and creative.

Chapter 24

Surah 24: Al Nur (The Light)

Sexual Laws (Surah 24:2-33)

The Qur'an contains practical instructions about sexual morality. Let's look at some of these instructions.

- What is the punishment for *zina* (adultery) and fornication? Ayat 2 says to flog each guilty person with 100 lashes, unmoved with compassion.

- How many witnesses are needed for a man to condemn a chaste woman? Unless he has four witnesses, he is subject to 80 lashes of flogging.

- A man can swear five times before Allah that his wife committed adultery. The wife can in turn swear five times that she is innocent.

- Anyone who has sinned sexually must marry someone else who is sexually impure.

- In public, men and women should lower their gaze in modesty. Women should cover themselves with clothing so that their beauty is hidden. They may only show themselves to "husbands, their fathers, their husband's fathers, their sons, their husband's sons, their brothers or their brother's sons, or their sister's sons, or their women, or the slaves whom their right hands possess, or male servants free of physical needs, or small children who have no sense of the shame of sex" (Surah 24:31).

- Ayat 58 says that slaves and children must ask permission to approach an adult Muslim before the morning prayer, at noon during the heat and after the evening prayer, because at these times people undress.

- Ayat 61 instructs good Muslims where they may eat meals. Similar to Ayat 31, they may eat with relatives and sincere friends, presumably other Muslims.

- Ayat 33 allows slaves to petition their masters for freedom. Muslims may free a slave if they think them worthy. Slave girls shouldn't be forced into prostitution, but it says, "if anyone compels them, yet, after such compulsion, if Allah Oft-Forgiving, Most Merciful."

My friends have asked why the Christian West is so immoral. Pointing to movies and music, they can find numerous examples.

The simple answer to my Muslim friends is that the West is *not* a Christian Empire. Isa did not come to set up an earthly kingdom. Yes, there are many followers of Isa in America, but they are the minority in government, the news media, sports, music, movies and television. The truth is opposite what you may think. Many Christians do not want to work in Hollywood because it is so godless! They realize that if they work in such a sexually charged environment, it might tempt them to fall into immorality like so many others. Only a person with great love for Isa can work in a place like Hollywood and be a faithful light for sexual purity.

Isa and his disciples taught sexual purity.

> But among you there must not be even a hint of sexual immorality, or of any kind of impurity, or of greed, because

these are improper for God's holy people. Nor should there be obscenity, foolish talk or coarse joking, which are out of place, but rather thanksgiving.[210]

The Injil teaches marriage between one man and one woman, condemns *all* sexual relationships before and outside of marriage and even warns against sexual fantasies in the heart. Isa's followers fight against abortion, prostitution, pornography, sexual abuse and many other sexual sins.

Why? Because Allah created sexuality as an amazing blessing to be enjoyed as part of sharing a life together. The intimacy between a husband and wife is part of a mirror to the perfect love found within Allah himself. When sexuality is expressed outside the bounds of a loving, life-long marriage, it quickly deteriorates into lust. Humans were originally created by Allah for pure relationships with him and with each other. To step outside these pure boundaries takes people into nothing but shadows and darkness.

Is there any hope? Including sexual sins committed deep in the heart and mind, does anyone live free of guilt? Viewed as a paragon of religious piety, Gandhi was known to have slept naked with beautiful young girls over many years of his life. He was supposedly doing an experiment to test his self-restraint. In doing so, he was admitting his struggle with desires to have sexual relations with many women.

Human efforts to overcome sexual brokenness fall short. Sexual sin needs Allah's forgiveness and healing. Even King Davud committed terrible sexual sin by committing adultery with the wife of one of his army officers. To make matters worse, Davud had the officer killed so he wouldn't discover she carried Davud's child.

Having become a dark shadow of his former self, Davud came before

---

[210] Injil, Ephesians 5:3-4

Allah asking for forgiveness and healing. "Create in me a clean heart," he cried, "and renew a right spirit in me."[211] In the end the specter of sexual sin steals all light from a person unless it is treated by Allah's cure. He looks for a broken and contrite heart that approaches the loving touch of Isa which is free of all lust and sensuality. His touch heals and brings joy everlasting.

---

[211] Zabur 51

Chapter 25

Surah 25: Al Furqan (The Criterion)

Is it Blasphemy to Call Allah Loving? (Surah 25:60)

The unbelievers may ask, "Who is Al Rahman (The Merciful)?" Even Muslims may wonder, "Who is Allah?"

One day a Christian lady met her Muslim friend to drink tea and talk about life. The Muslim lady told how difficult her life had been in her homeland where several armies had killed thousands of people and destroyed entire cities. The Christian woman sipped her tea and listened kindly. They both agreed that war is terrible and tragic. Wanting to encourage her friend, the Christian lady said, "You know, Allah loves you."

"Stop!" her friend suddenly burst out. "You must not say that, it's blasphemy! You can't talk about Allah like you would talk about a human."

These two ladies had different ideas about the question, "Who is Al Rahman?" The Christian believed, "Allah is the loving God who created our eyes and ears. Can't he see and hear us?"

The Muslim lady believed that Allah is so great and high above miserable humans that it was blasphemous to even mention Allah and then in the same breath say he loves us.

In Ayat 77, Muhammad is instructed to tell unbelievers that "My Lord is not uneasy because of you if ye call not on Him."

Does Al Rahman mean that Allah only *does* merciful things for humans, like sending rain to water the earth? Or does it mean that Allah is a personal being who actually loves humans with his will and affections? Allah has said, "I led them with cords of human kindness, with ties of love. To them I was like one who lifts a little child to the cheek, and I bent down to feed them."[212]

---

[212] Injil, Hosea 11:4

Chapter 26

Surah 26: Al Shuÿara' (The Poets)

Clear Meaning (Surah 26:2)

I started reading the Qur'an because I believe every person should use their Allah-given mind. I believe in both the necessity of divine revelation and human reason. Some Muslim friends say that hearing the sound of the Qur'an is like a breath of fresh air. Have I heard imams chanting the Qur'an? Yes, thousands of times. But I want to go to the next step of understanding the message.

One evening in a quiet park I brewed tea with our samovar. A nice Muslim family was picnicking at a table near us, so I walked over and offered them tea. While we talked and drank tea, I thought about Ayat like this one. "These are Verses of the Book that makes clear."

"Do you read the Qur'an?" I asked.

One of them answered, "We go to courses and learn how to read Arabic, but we don't understand what it says." The father agreed, "No, I don't understand it."

For many people, the message of the Qur'an is not clear. They turn to the *Tafsir* to explain what it means, they listen to their favorite imam or sheik. Sometimes in conversations about the Qur'an a hard question comes up and my friend quickly calls his teacher for the answer. Sometimes he already knows the answer, but wants the extra support from a higher authority. Sometimes he has no idea what to say.

Is a Tafsir necessary for reading through an interpretive translation of the Qur'an? People read the newspaper in their own language every day without a Tafsir.

One day I watched a popular Muslim imam teaching about a verse. He read the Ayat in plain language. But then he slowly and steadily explained how this word and that word didn't really mean what it clearly said. He said it means something else and then he explained that the whole sentence means something different than what he just read. Hundreds of Muslims sitting in the audience listened to their favorite imam while he took the clear meaning and moved away from it to an entirely different meaning.

Sitting and sipping tea with an older Muslim friend, another famous imam, I listened as he explained how the Muslims in North Africa and much of the Middle East are not true Muslims. I wondered, if the message of the Qur'an is clear, why do so many Muslims get it wrong?

"Why are there so many sects among the Christians?" my friends often ask me. "Is the message of the Injil clear or not?" The answer is that parts of the Injil are clear and part are not. Furthermore, some groups have elevated their traditions equal to or greater than the Injil. The ancient scholar Augustine said, "In the essentials unity, in the non-essentials liberty, in all things love." These essentials include agreement on the Oneness of Allah and forgiveness of sin through al-Masih.

When Muhammad first recited the Qur'an to the people of Mecca and Medina, he did not have a Tafsir. He apparently expected his audience to understand his plain message. After his death, his followers collected his sayings in the Hadith, but Muslims do not completely agree which are authentic and which are not. So they cannot be considered equal in authority to the Qur'an, which all Muslims accept.

If the message of the Qur'an is clear—and I think it is so far—then shouldn't people read it and rely less on the opinions of strangers?

Chapter 27

Surah 27: Al Naml (The Ants)

Bowing to Allah's Will (Surah 27:91)

Muhammad declares in Ayat 91, "I am commanded to be of those who bow in Islam to Allah's Will."

The word Islam means *submission*. When an army wins the battle, their enemies must submit. They must bow low in the dust to show they are conquered. According to the Qur'an, Allah conquers rebellious people. Sometimes he destroys people and sometimes he turns them into good Muslims.

What are Allah's reasons for creating the world and allowing it to fill up with rebellious people? Couldn't he have simply created a world where everyone bowed to his will in submission? What makes some people go astray? Why bother to create rebellious people who would land in the fires of Hell when he could have only created good Muslims prepared for Paradise?

Why does Allah want slaves to work in his fields? Slaves provide labor for their master. They dig and harvest, hammer and build. Their master uses them to accomplish something for himself, to do something he cannot do alone.[213] The Pharaohs used slaves to build the great pyramids because they personally couldn't budge the large rocks and their free citizens didn't want to be bothered with the manual labor.

No one believes Allah made human slaves because he needed their help. Islam requires Muslims to establish justice and Faith in the earth. But why is it so hard? Why does it involve striving physically and spiritually? Why would Allah ever give his slaves the power to revolt against his will? Even the Pharaohs and the Caesars kept their slaves under absolute control. Musa led the Hebrew slaves to freedom but only by the miraculous power of Allah. If human masters can control their slaves, why has Allah allowed so many of his slaves to boldly rebel and blaspheme and mock him?

From the Injil's point of view, these questions are unnecessary. Adam and Hawwa were first created in friendship with Allah. After the friendship was broken they became slaves of sin. Then Allah gave the children of Isra'il strict rules. But Isa ended servanthood and restored friendship with Allah. In love he laid down his own life for his friends.

---

[213] Surah 29:6, "And if any strive (with might and main), they do so for their own souls: for Allah is free of all needs from all creation."

Chapter 28

Surah 28: Al Qasas (The Narrations)

Who Does Allah Love? (Surah 28:76)

The Qur'an recounts the stories of Musa and Nuh many times. The essence of the message is the same. Those who rebel again Allah will be destroyed. Those who believe and practice good works will be saved.

Ayat 76 says, "Allah loveth not those who exult." The Qur'an asserts that Allah does not love sinners. As discussed, it is not clear that Allah loves anyone in the way we think of love. Some people even consider it blasphemy to say he does.

If Allah does not love a sinner, does his attitude toward the person change if he repents? Imagine an atheist who loves money. It seems from this Ayat that Allah does not love the worldly atheist. He should be told, "Allah does not love you." If he repents and becomes a Muslim, should he be told "Now Allah loves you?"

If so, has the former atheist earned Allah's love? This could be called conditional love, or "I love you if" love. For example, a man tells his wife, "I love you if you have sex with me any time I want." What happens if his wife doesn't always feel like he does? What

> Unconditional love simply says, "I love you."

happens if she becomes ill for several months? Does he divorce her and find another wife? What if he says, "I love you if you produce a child for me?" After a few years of marriage with no baby he tells her, "No child, no love. I divorce you." I know a family where just this thing happened.

Conditional love is typical among humans. We love those who love us. We love those who do something for us.

Someone might say, "Allah loves good people because they do what he wants. They obey him." This means he loves people who earn his love. Unconditional love simply says, "I love you." It doesn't depend on how anyone behaves. A husband with this special love, called agape love, tells his wife "Maybe you can't have children, but I still love you and will never leave you." The Injil demonstrates agape love when Isa was willing to die for his enemies. He loved everyone.

Chapter 29

Surah 29: Al Ankabut (The Spider)

How Can We Do Anything Good? (Surah 29:7)

One day a son approached his father and said, "Father, my car engine is broken. It is so weak I can't even drive home with a bag of rice."

The father listened silently, thinking about a solution. He answered, "True, you need a new engine. I will pay for a new engine if you can first transport it home in your car."

Do you see the impossibility of this solution? Presented this choice, the son has no way of ever getting a new engine. Why? Because his old engine is defective. It is too weak. How can he use his old engine to get a new one?

If I tell someone, "Allah will blot out the evil in you, but first you must believe in him and do righteous deeds,"[214] this is like the father telling

---

[214] Surah 29:7, "Those who believe and work righteous deeds, from them shall We blot out all evil in them, And We shall reward them according to the best of their deeds."

his son to bring home the new engine in his broken car. The evil resident in our hearts makes us too weak to do truly righteous deeds that would renew us.

We try to be sexually chaste (remember Gandhi) but our hearts and eyes wander with lust. We try to be generous, but underneath the surface our hearts are ravenous wolves always greedy for more. We try to do prayers, but we get distracted by the glitter of this world. We try to strive for justice, but we prefer the comfort of our couches. Our best efforts are insufficient.

The gloomy son looks at his father and says, "Please Father, I can't bring the new engine home, no matter how hard I try."

The father, if a loving one, says with a smile, "Of course child, let's go together and I'll pay to install a new engine in your car today. Then you can haul off the old engine and toss it in the rubbish pile."

In this case the son depends 100% on his father's gift of love. He offers no work or effort in the resurrection of his car. His only response is to trust his father.

The Same Allah? (Surah 29:46)

We've read that Jews and Christians (People of the Book) are considered guilty of shirk because they worship other gods besides Allah. The Jews are accused of worshipping Uzair and the Christians are accused of lifting up Miriam and Isa as Allah's associates.

The Qur'an calls shirk one of the greatest sins. We've read that the punishment for shirk is the fires of Hell. Muslims are commanded to subdue the Jews and Christians until they pay the jizyah and feel themselves subdued under the rule of Islam in the land. Anyone who commits shirk is a *mushrik* (polytheist). Perhaps there was some hope for the Jews and Christians who had never heard of Islam, but those who have heard Muhammad's message and rejected it are numbered among the transgressors.

Suddenly in 29:16 we encounter an amazingly dissimilar passage.

> And dispute ye not with the people of the Book, except
> with means better, unless it be with those of them who
> inflict wrong: but say, "We believe in the Revelation which
> has come down to us and in that which came down to you;
> our God and your God is One; and it is to Him we bow."

This is complicated. How can this Ayat mean that Muslims, when they
bow in their mosques, are bowing to the same Allah Christians worship
in their churches and Jews bow to in their synagogues? Even if Jews,
Christians and Muslims worship the same Allah in a general sense,
wouldn't Allah still punish the People of the Book for associating
partners with him? Is this Ayat now telling us that Jews and Christians
are not guilty of polytheism? If so, then I must agree, but ask why the
complete turnaround?

Moreover, this Ayat endorses the Tawrat, Prophets and Injil. It
doesn't say they have been corrupted, but are worthy of trust.

Several years ago on a long ferryboat ride a friendly passenger
approached me. We introduced ourselves and chatted together. He
complimented our children and then asked, "Have you looked into
Islam?"

"Yes, I have read some of the Qur'an and studied Islam. I've also
studied the earlier revelation."

"Did you know we worship the same Allah and share many prophets?
I can't even be a good Muslim unless I love the prophet Isa. It would
make me so happy if you would become a Muslim."

I thanked him for his polite words about my children and we said
goodbye at the port.

Do we all worship Allah? Let's be careful here. Many Christian friends
have also asked me the same question. Is Yahweh (יְהוָה) in the Tawrat,

Theos (θεός) in the Injil and Allah (الله) in the Qur'an the same Person? Jews say that Yahweh sent Musa and Davud, but not Isa and not Muhammad. Christians believe all the Tawrat, Prophets and the Injil, but do not accept Muhammad as a messenger. This is not to be critical, just to state the obvious.

If we say Jews, Christians and Muslims all believe in an ultimate Creator, that much is true. But it cannot mean that they believe the same things about him. Who is Allah? Each faith answers the question differently. If not, they would all be one faith.

This discussion gets more complicated when we jump ahead to Surah 109.

> Say: O ye that reject Faith! I worship not that which ye worship, Nor will ye worship that which I worship. And I will not worship that which ye have been wont to worship, Nor will ye worship that which I worship. To you be your Way, and to me mine.

This sounds more like the standard belief of Islam. It rejects all other religions. Polytheism in any form is incompatible with the core Islamic doctrine of Tawhid.

Added to the different beliefs about Allah is the difference in religious practices. Muslims have Five Pillars: *Shahada, Salat, Zakat, Sawm* and *Hajj*. Jews and Christians have different confessions and different worship practices. The contrasting beliefs and practices must place Jews, Christians and Muslims in separate categories.

Imagine two friends have a chat about the king of their land. One of them is convinced their king is a dashing young man, unmarried with no children. The other believes the king is a gray-haired grandfather. The first thinks the king fought in two wars, but the second thinks the king has always been a man of peace. Both are correct that their country has a king. Both could be wrong about the details of his identity, but they certainly can't both be right.

Our conversation is about someone far greater than a human king. Allah is the sovereign over all the universe. He created it and shares it with the human race, allowing us to build computers, eat pomegranates and produce families. It is critical we know the truth about this divine King. Everything depends on knowing his true identity.

Chapter 30

Surah 30: Al Rum (The Romans)

Islamic Sects (Surah 30:32)

The Qur'an frowns upon sects. It says,

> Those who split up their Religion, and become Sects, each party rejoicing in that which is with itself!

History shows lethal conflict in early Islam. After the death of Muhammad three of his first four Caliphs were assassinated. They were Umar ibn al-Khattab, Uthman ibn 'Affan, and Ali ibn Abi-Talib.

In later years many sects developed within the Sunni and Shiite branches. The Sunnis have five schools of jurisprudence (*madhhad*): *Hanafi, Maliki, Shafi'i, Hanbali* and *Ẓāhirī*. Shiites have Fivers, Seveners and Twelvers. Qarmatians, Ismailis, Fatimids, Assassins of Alamut and Druses all emerged from the Seveners. Isma'ilism later split into Nizari Ismaili and Musta'li Ismaili, and then Mustaali was divided into Hafizi and Taiyabi Ismailis. Moreover, Imami-Shi'a later brought into existence Ja'fari jurisprudence. There are also Akhbarism, Usulism, Shaykism, Alawites and Alevism were all developed from Ithna'asharis.

This is just a small part of the list. Still, Muslims share in common the Shahada and belief in the Qur'an.

Christians too have many sects and have sometimes seen violence against one another contrary to Isa's teaching. There are Roman Catholics and Eastern Orthodox. Five hundred years ago the Protestant Reformation created a new movement of churches independent of the Roman Pope. Among the Protestants many more sub-groups developed. Some of these churches were distinguished by language and social class, while others separated over disagreements in belief. Despite many questions about things like church organization, Isa's second coming or the best kind of pastor, Christians look to Isa al-Masih as the Savior from sin.

What is it in human nature that makes us gravitate toward schisms rather than unity?

Chapter 31

Surah 31: Luqman

Filling the Earth with Words (Surah 31:27)

This poetic passage says,

> And if all the trees on earth were pens and the Ocean (were ink), with seven Oceans behind it to add to its, yet would not the Words of Allah be exhausted for Allah is Exalted in power, full of Wisdom.

We've established that there is one Kalimatullah. In Isa al-Masih Allah spoke His Word to a dying world. If all the world was filled with the Words of Allah, would this not bring special focus upon the Kalimatullah?

Isa's follower John wrote, "Jesus did many other things as well. If every one of them were written down, I suppose that even the whole world would not have room for the books that would be written."[215] Oceans of ink would not suffice to tell about all the wonderful love and deeds of Isa Kalimatullah.

---

[215] Injil, John 21:25

Chapter 32

Surah 32: Al Sajdah (The Prostration)

Destined for Hell (Surah 32:13)

My eyes grow weary of trying to peer into the depths of the human heart. Does the heart have a free-will? Does anyone have a choice about their future? Can anyone freely choose to follow Allah or not? Has Allah chiseled the fate of every human soul into an immutable slab of granite?

Ayat 13 says, "If We had so willed we could certainly have brought every soul its true guidance: but the World from Me will come true, I will fill Hell with Jinns and men all together."

For centuries Christians have tried to understand the relationship between Allah's sovereign will and human free-will. Can a person freely choose to repent and believe in Isa al-Masih? If not, why would Allah create some people for the purpose of tossing them like a piece of coal into the fire-pits of Hell?

Most Christians have answered this question by affirming both the love of Allah and the free-will of individuals. They say that Allah desired a relationship with creatures who would freely love and obey him. If love is under compulsion, it isn't love at all. A man can never force a woman to love him. The moment he uses force the love is forever shattered like a broken cup.

If Allah wanted true love from his human creatures, he could not force them to love him. He could have willed everyone to be sinless, just like he created the angels. Without the ability to freely love Allah or not, would we be truly human?

Chapter 33

Surah 33: Al Ahzab (The Confederates)

The Life of Muhammad (Surah 33)

Much has been written about Surah 33 in other books. I just want make a couple of comments here.

First, adoption is not a Muslim practice. One day Muhammad caught a glimpse of the wife of his foster son Zayd. Her name was Zeynip. Zayd divorced Zeynip and then Muhammad married her. In Islam adoption does not exist, so there is never the problem of a Muslim man unable to marry the former wife of an adopted son. Ayat 37,

> We joined her in marriage to thee: in order that there may
> be no difficulty to the Believers in marriage with the wives
> of their adopted sons, when the latter have dissolved.

Second, Ayat 50 grants Muhammad permission to an unlimited number of believing women, slave-girls captured in battle, cousins on both sides of his family and other women. History shows that Muhammad had at least 11 wives, 4 concubines and four divorces. Zeynip was Muhammad's fifth wife. This Ayat gave him permission to take more than the four wife limit prescribed to ordinary Muslim men in Surah 4:3. I have been surprised over the years how many people fail to realize this simple fact of history.

"Did the movie show all the wives of Muhammad?" I asked my good friend after he saw a movie about the Muslim prophet.

He looked at me very oddly and paused. "What do you mean?" he asked.

"I'm sorry, didn't you know about all the wives of Muhammad after Khadija?"

"No, he only had one wife," he insisted, becoming slightly irritated.

"I thought all Muslims knew about his wives. It's no secret after all," I said. We went on to discuss this basic fact which he had never heard in spite of being a pious young man.

Third, people had to be careful not to annoy Muhammad. Ayat 57 says, "Those who annoy Allah and His Messenger- Allah has cursed them in this world and in the Hereafter, and has prepared for them a humiliating Punishment." This passage says that sometimes guests would come to Muhammad's home for a meal. They stayed too long and talked too much. Muhammad was embarrassed to tell them to leave, but with an Ayat, Allah warned the Muslims to avoid annoying him.

Chapter 34

Surah 34: Saba' (Sheba)

More Warnings (Surah 34)

The Qur'an asserts that Muhammad was not possessed by a spirit and that he was not a liar. Many passages defend Muhammad as a real messenger of Allah. The unbelievers and hypocrites had their reasons to reject his message. They demanded signs and Muhammad said that nothing more would be given except the Ayat in the Qur'an. They said he was just telling old fables, but he replied that his message was a fresh revelation from Allah that confirmed the Earlier Books. He warned them sternly and in detail how terrible their punishment would be on the Day of Judgment. They laughed but he said it would certainly come upon them.

Chapter 35

Surah 35: Fatir (The Originator of Creation)

Not a Soul Left Alive (Surah 35:45)

This passage jumped off the page at me. This agrees with the Injil. All people are guilty at some level. What makes humans stray into rebellion? How could Allah's good creation turn so sour?

> If Allah were to punish men according to what they deserve, He would not leave on the back of the...a single living creature:

Many years ago my friend told me this story. An honest judge presided over a city. One day the police brought him a young man in the courthouse. He was guilty of speeding through the city center, endangering everyone. The judge looked up. Sadly, his gaze fell upon his own flesh and blood son. He loved his him, but he also loved justice.

"Are you guilty?" the judge asked from behind his high bench.

The son hung his head low. "Yes, your honor."

"Then as a just judge of this city, I pronounce you guilty and sentence you to 30 days in prison or a fine of $10,000."

"Yes, your honor." The son feared to raise his eyes before his judge and father.

Suddenly the judge stood to his feet, stepped away from his high bench and removed his black robe. "As your judge I condemned you. As your father, I forgive you." He stepped down from the high table and walked to the police officer. "Here, I will pay the fine myself."

This parable shows something about Allah. His justice requires him to punish our sin. If Ayat 45 is correct—and I believe it is—that every human is guilty of violating Allah's laws and therefore deserves death, then Allah would not be just if he failed to give a punishment. Imagine the judge looking at his son and saying, "I don't care if you are guilty, you may go without any consequence."

If we are guilty and Allah is loving and just, he must provide a solution that provides for our forgiveness while pouring out his just wrath upon our wrongdoing.

Chapter 36

Surah 36: Ya Sin

Condemned (Surah 36:6)

One of the core ideas expressed in the Qur'an is that Allah sent Muhammad to the polytheistic Arabs because they were living in darkness. They had no prophet, no book, no signs and no knowledge of Allah. The Arabs were not Jewish or Christian. The people of Mecca had filled the Ka'aba with idols.

However, Muslims also believe that long ago Ibrahim and Ismail traveled to Mecca and built the Ka'aba. History shows that the Arabs knew about Allah before Muhammad was born. Muhammad's father was named Abdullah. The Syriac Christians living in Arabia used the title Al Rahmana for Isa. The stories of Nuh, Lut, Ibrahim, Musa, Davud and Suleiman had spread widely among tribal people, nomads and traders roaming the deserts.

What is the purpose of the Qur'an according to Ayat 6?

> In order that thou mayest admonish a people, whose fathers had received no admonition, and who therefore

remain heedless.

This Ayat does not say that the Tawrat, Prophets and Injil were corrupted. It says that the Arab fathers had not received admonition. But what about the knowledge of the Ka'aba which we are told was built by the prophet Ibrahim?

On the other hand, if the Arabs had received revelation about Allah before they got the Qur'an—and it is certain that they already knew about Allah as the supreme Creator—why does Ayat 6 speak as though the Arabs were clueless about the truth?

Let's say that the Arabs had never heard of Allah or any of his books. Living without any revelation, they turned to idols. If they had no knowledge of Allah and his will, why would they be guilty?

One day we sat in my friend's living room talking about the Injil and Allah. He asked me, "Would it be fair for Allah to condemn someone for doing something he or she didn't know was wrong?" He continued, "If Allah doesn't condemn people unless they reject him, wouldn't it be better to leave the pagans alone so they will never be guilty of rejecting Allah? If you tell them Allah exists, you are actually doing something worse than leaving them in darkness."

I'm sure Muslim scholars have their answers to these questions. The Injil answers the question in this way. Allah has revealed his existence through his creation. The splendor, design, and beauty of the universe point to a Creator. Secondly, the Injil says that Allah has written his law of right and wrong on human hearts. Everyone has a conscience that either accuses or excuses them. The Good News (Injil) is that Isa did not come into the world to condemn the world, but that through him the world might be saved.

Chapter 37

Surah 37: Al Saffat (Those Ranged in Ranks)

The Momentous Ransom Sacrifice (Surah 37:102-107)

Few stories grip us like Ibrahim offering his son as a sacrifice on the mountain. It first appears in the Tawrat. Allah visits Ibrahim and tells him to take his son to the mountain and kill him there as a burnt sacrifice.

The story is unthinkable. What internal torment did Ibrahim go through? He would have to slay his own tender, beloved son of promise and then stand patiently watching the fire slowly consume his flesh and hair. How could Ibrahim bear the thought of his heart breaking into a million pieces as he looked into those innocent, trusting eyes? Such was the ultimate test of faith.

The Qur'an does not name the son, but the Tawrat names Isak, the miracle son of Ibrahim and his wife Sara. Obeying Allah's command, Ibrahim took Isak and two servants and traveled three days to the mountain of sacrifice. When they arrived, Ibrahim instructed the servants to wait below. He took wood and led Isak up the mountain slope.

"Father?" Isak asked.

"Here am I, my son." Can we hear Ibrahim's voice crack with agony?

"You have a fire and wood, but where is the lamb for the burnt offering?"

Ibrahim replied, "My son, Allah himself will provide a lamb for a burnt offering."

On the mountain Ibrahim built an altar, covered it with wood, tied his son and laid him on it. Then he lifted the knife to kill his son.

Just then, an angel called to him, "Ibrahim, Ibrahim!"

"Here I am," he answered.

"Don't do anything to the boy, now I know that you fear Allah because you have not withheld your son, your only son from me."

Ibrahim looked up and saw a ram caught in the thicket. The tangled horns left him no escape. Ibrahim caught the ram and in the place of his son, he offered it as a burnt offering. To remember Allah's gift he named the place, *Yahweh Yireh*, meaning "Allah provides."[216]

Any loving father or mother prefers not to dwell on the details of this story. When a child falls ill, what parent doesn't wish he or she could take away their pain, even take their place? Who can bear the thought of losing a child? Yet Allah tells Ibrahim to do the impossible.

We need to find two very important pieces to this puzzle. First, what did Ibrahim expect Allah to do for him if he sacrificed Isak? Second, what is the significance of the ram caught in the bush?

Solving this puzzle starts with a promise. Isak was no ordinary son. He was born because Allah did a miracle in an old man and woman.

---

[216] Tawrat, Genesis 22

But more than that, Isak was the son of the Promise. Allah promised that he would grow to be a man and have a vast number of descendants, more than the stars in the sky or the sands of the sea.[217] When Allah told Ibrahim to offer Isak upon the altar as a sacrifice, this appeared to contradict the promise that he would become a great man and father of nations. How could a dead and cremated child have a future? Impossible!

Maybe not. Ibrahim had extraordinary faith in the promises of Allah. Here's the solution to the puzzle.

> By faith Abraham, when God tested him, offered Isaac as a sacrifice. He who had embraced the promises was about to sacrifice his one and only son, even though God had said to him, "It is through Isaac that your offspring will be reckoned." Abraham reasoned that God could even raise the dead, and so in a manner of speaking he did receive Isaac back from death.[218]

Ibrahim was willing to go through with the unthinkable because he trusted Allah to raise Isak back to life, cause him to grow into a strong man and become the father of nations.

But why put Ibrahim through the torment? Yes, Allah tested his faith. Still, we need another piece of the puzzle.

Surah 37:107 says, "We ransomed him with a momentous sacrifice." The Tawrat agrees, Allah rescued Isak from certain death by sending a substitute. Allah accepted the ram in place of the boy.

Here is the second part of the solution to the puzzle. The ransom for

---

[217] Tawrat, Genesis 17:19, "Then God said, 'Yes, but your wife Sarah will bear you a son, and you will call him Isaac. I will establish my covenant with him as an everlasting covenant for his descendants after him.'"

[218] Injil, Hebrews 11:17-19

Ibrahim's son is a parable of the greatest substitutionary sacrifice. Think of it. Allah could have let Isak experience the ordeal of dying, being burned and then coming back to life. Instead, Allah was satisfied to accept the sacrifice in his place.

We have already noticed that the best sacrifice is the one Allah prepares himself. He sacrificed the first animals to cover Adam and Hawwa's shame. He met Musa in a bush that he ignited with holy fire. For Ibrahim and his son he provided a ram.

On the way up the mountainside Ibrahim told his son, "Allah will provide a lamb." He spoke those words as a prophecy. Thousands of years later, Allah provided his Lamb, the perfect and final sacrifice.

The prophet Yeshaya said al-Masih, "was led like a lamb to the slaughter, and as a sheep before its shearers is silent, so he did not open his mouth." All of us have strayed from Allah like wayward sheep, but he has put all our iniquity on the perfect Lamb.[219]

> On the way up the mountainside Ibrahim told his son, "Allah will provide a lamb."

With these two essential pieces of the puzzle, the picture is much clearer. Ibrahim believed Allah would raise the son of Promise from the dead making him father of nations and this story is a parable of the greatest sacrifice who would ransom us from sin.

---

[219] Prophets, Yeshaya 53:6-7

Chapter 38

Surah 38: Sad

More about Heaven (Surah 38:49-53)

One day a Muslim and a Christian talked about the afterlife. The Christian said he hopes to reach Heaven and the Muslim said he looks forward to a place called Paradise. Though both concepts describe the afterlife, they are not identical. What is the afterlife like? Who will be there? The two friends shared their different beliefs.

As often happens, the subject of virgin girls (*houris*) came up in the discussion. The Muslim said, "I think you Christians are jealous of our Islamic Paradise, that's why you always bring up the houris."

The other man replied, "No, we aren't jealous. What could be more pleasing and glorious than living face-to-face with our beloved Allah in his holy presence?"

Surah 38 goes into more detail about the rewards of the Islamic Paradise. The Qur'an promises good believers (mumin) a place flowing with strong drink that never intoxicates, rivers of purest water and women with beautiful eyes. Perhaps these images are symbolic. Is this just a poetic way of saying that Paradise is extraordinarily comfortable and pleasurable? I'm just not sure.

These verses could be literal. We have seen that the Qur'an allows Muslim men to take up to four wives and as many concubines as they wish. It would not be a contradiction for Allah to allow men to have multiple sexual partners in Paradise, assuming they are treated fairly. How then will Muslim women be treated in Paradise?

Standing at this intersection, I am faced with roads going in opposite directions. Isa al-Masih said, "For when they shall rise from the dead, they neither marry, nor are given in marriage; but are as the angels which are in heaven." Christians believe that sex and child-bearing belong to this life only. In Heaven men and women will no longer have sexual relationships. They will exchange the fleeting pleasures of sexuality for the eternal pleasures of enjoying holy friendship with one another and with Allah as they glorify him forever.

Chapter 39

Surah 39: Al Zumar (Crowds)
And
Surah 40: Ghafir (Forgiver)
or Al Mu'min (The Believer)

More Rewards and Judgment (Surahs 39 and 40)

Our reading is speeding up with shorter and shorter Surahs. Unbelievers are frequently warned that they will enter the perilous fires of Hell. Believers are encouraged that they will enter Paradise with crowds of others. The contrast is huge. Fires in Hell. Rivers of Water in Paradise. The Jinn and unbelievers will suffer immense torment. The angels and believers will enjoy delicious pleasures.

One evening my family sat with some close Muslim friends. The conversation turned to the afterlife. We wondered, "What will the Muslim Paradise be like? How does the Injil describe Heaven?"

Our friend said, "With rivers and gardens, I think Paradise is a lovely place, what do you think?"

"Sounds lovely," I answered. "I just have a question. Do you hope to see Allah, to have a close relationship with him?"

"That's hard to answer," they answered. "What does the Injil say?'

To answer to this question I thought back to my childhood. My grandmother died in her late 60's from serious lung problems. She was one of my favorite people, always full of love and lots of smiles. My mother wept to lose her mother and we all felt the cloud of sadness in the following days. During the funeral week my parents arranged for me to stay with my great-aunt and great-uncle.

One afternoon my great-aunt saw me sitting alone in the living room, feeling sad and bored. She sat down beside me and said, "May I show you something special? Your grandmother is gone now, but we can see her again in Heaven."

She got my attention.

"Listen to these words about Heaven," she said, opening the Injil.

> And I heard a loud voice from the throne saying, "Look! God's dwelling place is now among the people, and he will dwell with them. They will be his people, and God himself will be with them and be their God. 'He will wipe every tear from their eyes. There will be no more death' or mourning or crying or pain, for the old order of things has passed away."[220]

I listened to her gentle voice and gazed out a huge window into a large garden behind their house. A giant magnolia tree stood on the left, lifting branches to the sky like a ladder. Green grass stretched far to the back where her husband had planted a lush vegetable patch. Just at the garden's edge mighty pine trees abruptly soared above everything else.

---

[220] Injil, Revelation 21:3-4

My great-aunt continued talking. "When Isa al-Masih returns, he will make everything new. A city measuring thousands of kilometers will descend out of Heaven. Stones like pure gold and jasper will make up its walls. The foundations will consist of stones like topaz, beryl and amethyst. The gates will be pearls and the streets gold like transparent glass."

Dazzling gemstones filled my imagination. She read on.

> I did not see a temple in the city, because the Lord God Almighty and the Lamb are its temple. The city does not need the sun or the moon to shine on it, for the glory of God gives it light, and the Lamb is its lamp.[221]

Later that week my parents took me home, but the next day we got more unexpected news. My great-aunt had died in her sleep.

Can you see what happened within me that quiet afternoon when my grandmother died? Gazing at my great-aunt's lush garden, hearing about Heaven, thinking about life and death, I realized something that changed me forever. Someday, like every Christian, I will make a great exchange. I will exchange these sensual desires for spiritual ones. No longer satisfied with earthy pleasures, I will find my true satisfaction living in the presence of Allah. Heaven is Allah's home. It will someday be ours too. What more could I ever want?

---

[221] Injil, Revelation 21:22-23

Chapter 40

Surah 41:
Fussilat (Expounded) or Ha Mim

Why Does Evil Exist? (Surah 41:49)

The story of Adam and Hawwa starts with the truth that Allah is loving and all-powerful. And yet, evil exists in the world. Not only do people harm one another by lying, cheating, misusing sexuality and murdering, but earthquakes crumble houses and tsunamis wash away cities full of innocent people.

Surah 41:49 says, "Man does not weary of asking for good, but if ill touches him, he gives up all hope, is lost in despair." This Ayat proves that people of all time sometimes lose faith in Allah's goodness when they experience pain. They ponder, "If Allah loves me, why did my family die in the earthquake?"

I sat with my friends sharing cups of Arab coffee. We talked and laughed as their little children entertained us. Their four-month-old baby was strong and chubby, just like he should be. Everyone enjoyed bouncing him on their laps.

But our conversation became very hushed when our friend starting telling about losing her family in a war. Only 25 years old, she had to bury her innocent little sons and daughters. Before the funeral, she took some pictures of them.

> Why does evil exist?

One by one we passed around her cell phone and looked at the heart-wrenching photos. Her tender little daughter was wrapped in a white blanket, making it look as though she was just taking an afternoon nap. Her face was pure and sweet.

The next picture showed her little boy. Apparently he was killed by an exploding bomb. Shrapnel lacerated his face and body. He was still dressed in play clothes. Maybe he was kicking a ball outside his home when the bomb exploded. His head was turned to the side and in spite of the bloody marks on his face, he seemed to be resting peacefully.

Unable to look any longer, I handed the phone back to our friend. The bombs didn't touch my children, but how could I harden my heart at the sight of her dead loved ones?

On a different occasion, a friend raised his voice and angrily demanded I explain to him why Allah had allowed a girls dormitory to go up in flames while they had no way to escape. Someone had locked the doors so the girls wouldn't sneak out. The deaths of the teenage girls touched hundreds of loving family members and friends. He raised his voice and demanded to know, "You say Allah exists. You say he parted the Red Sea for the children of Ibrahim and that he raised Isa from the dead. Tell me, was it too hard a thing for him to turn the key and unlock one insignificant door for those girls to escape? Tell me!"

In the last hundred years several writers have become famous and wealthy for asking hard questions that accuse Allah. If Allah is all-powerful and loving, why doesn't he stop suffering? When bad things touch a man, "he gives up all hope." Those who lose hope in Allah find solace in sharing their hopelessness and bitterness with one another.

One day on Facebook I posted the question, "What do you think? How can a loving Allah allow humans to suffer and evil to exist?" Several friends answered.

"Because of free will," one wrote.

Another said, "I reckon if Allah were to intervene and prevent every human act that would do harm, folks would be asking, 'If Allah is both good and all powerful, why does he keep us all as slaves against our will?'"

One friend listened but still felt dissatisfied. She said, "Some people are too caught up in wanting 'answers'. Allah is infinite, and eternal, and there's no way we can understand his perspective."

"Do you think Allah himself understands the problem?" I responded.

"Yes, of course he knows what he's doing, but I don't think it's as straightforward as a simplistic logical 'answer'. We all see a little piece of the huge tapestry—to use a very flawed analogy—and there's probably a grain of truth in all the standard 'answers', but none of them contains the whole truth. They can't. Our minds cannot comprehend the vastness of Allah's perspective."

"Allah's mind is far greater than ours," I agreed.

"Anyway, I think when people ask the questions about suffering and evil in the world, they're not looking for a logical answer anyway."

"What do you think they are looking for?" I asked.

"Either they're making excuses for not meeting with Isa al-Masih or they are hurting so much that they simply need to know they're loved, and that Allah is in some sense hurting with them."

My friends all agreed. Allah did not stand at a distance from our suffering. Through al-Masih he entered our suffering at the deepest level. The Injil reassures us, "For we have not an high priest which cannot be touched with the feeling of our infirmities; but was in all points tempted like as we are, yet without sin."[222]

---

[222] Injil, Hebrews 4:15. "High Priest" is a special title used in the Injil for al-Masih. It means that he presents the perfect sacrifice, in this case his own life, as a substitution for us, taking the penalty of our sin upon himself. He is both High Priest and Lamb of Allah.

Chapter 41

Surah 42: Al Shura (Consultation)

Does Allah Speak to People? (Surah 42:51)

The Qur'an says that the angel Jibril spoke to Muhammad. While affirming that Allah wants to speak to people, Surah 42:51 introduces more ways that he speaks.

> It is not fitting for a man that Allah should speak to him except by inspiration or from behind a veil, or by the sending of a Messenger to reveal, with Allah's permission, what Allah wills.

Does this mean that Allah spoke to or still speaks to people without sending them a messenger? What is inspiration or speech behind the veil? It's a fascinating question.

After communism failed in Central Asia, the Muslim peoples living there began to learn about Allah again. For 70 years the Communists told them that Allah is a fairy tale for old women and little children.

In the Talas river valley a Kazakh family began reading the Qur'an and Injil. Former Communists brought the police to their house and demanded to know what they believed. They also brought along two imams, one young and one old. The former Communists rejected all religions and the imams distrusted the Injil.

All of them sat on the floor in their salon, the atmosphere very tense. The police and imams demanded to know why they were studying the Injil. The young imam ridiculed them for talking about Isa al-Masih.

The wife patiently explained, "Didn't you know that the Qur'an talks about al-Masih?"

"No it doesn't, that's a kafir religion," the young imam said, scolding them.

"But here are Ayat that talk about him," she said, holding an open Qur'an for everyone to see.

The older imam turned to his younger apprentice, motioning to be quiet. "She's right, you know."

What started this family on the quest for Allah? It started partly because the wife saw an unforgettable dream. When she woke up, she knew without a doubt that Allah had sent her an inspiration.

What was special about her dream? She saw the tallest mountains of the world, with everything bending down before them far into the horizon. Above the mountains a light blazed out of the sky and in the light stood a being in the shape of a man, clothed in robes whiter than purest snow. Blazing light emitted from the person's face, pouring down in blinding waves like the greatest waterfall. She marveled at his blindingly white face and robes. An inner voice told her she was looking at Isa al-Masih in his resurrection glory. His glory reigned over all.

Reports come in every week from around the globe. This person in purest white visits people in dreams and visions. He inspires people to awake and begin their search for the truth (*al Hak*).

Chapter 42

Surah 43: Al Zukhruf (The Gold Adornments)

A Book in Arabic (Surah 43:3)

> "We have made it a Qur'an in Arabic, that ye may be able to understand."

The world has over 20,000 languages. Which one is the hardest to learn? The English language has the largest vocabulary with over a million words. Chinese, Tamil, Turkish, Russian and many others have large vocabularies and complicated grammar. Arabic too is complicated to both speak and read. Again we come to an Ayat that says the Qur'an was given in Arabic for people who could understand it. In the 1400 years since the Qur'an came the percentage of the world's population that understands Arabic is still small, maybe smaller than ever. Only 3% of the world's population speaks in Arabic. If the Qur'an was given for everyone, why did it come in a language so few understand?

Someone might ask the same thing about the Injil. It was written in

Greek, but even fewer people today understand that ancient language. The answer is that Christians believe the message is more important than the original language.

The Return of Isa al-Masih (Surah 43:61)

"We believe Isa is coming again, just like you do!" My friend smiled happily at the thought. "When he comes back he will clear away all false religion and establish Islam throughout the earth before the Last Day."

My first response was a simple question. "If Isa is coming back before the Last Day and setting everything right, wouldn't that make him the last prophet?"

I have asked that question many times and no one can give an easy answer. But why do Muslims look for the Second Coming of Isa anyway? The Qur'an is not clear. It says, "And shall be a Sign the Hour. Therefore have no doubt about the, but follow ye Me: this is a Straight Way." Commentators like to add their own words, but we are not doing that.

Does the Injil speak of Isa's Second Coming? Yes, in great detail. It warns of difficult days before his coming. The earth will be filled with battles and wars, nations clashing with one another, pestilence, earthquakes and sorrows around the earth. People will rise against Isa's followers in hatred, falsely accusing them, persecuting and killing them.[223] Isa said that false prophets and false Masihs would arise in various places. Meanwhile, in spite of all these things, the Good News (Injil) would be spoken to all the nations before the Last Day.

Just as the world collapses deeper into darkness, a great deceiver will

---

[223] In the early 21st century more than a million Christians were killed for their faith around the world.

arise and take his stand in a most holy place, compelling all the nations to worship him. This false Masih will succeed for just a few years. Then the true Masih will return and establish his just kingdom of peace.[224] He will sit as judge of the living and dead. Like separating sheep and goats, Isa will separate his people from unbelievers. The ones spiritually unborn will pass into everlasting death while his born again people will pass into everlasting life.

Do Christians believe in the Last Day? Absolutely. We say yes and amen. *Maranatha*, Come quickly Masih Isa.

---

[224] Injil, Matthew 24

Chapter 43

Surah 44: Al Dukhan (The Smoke)
And
Surah 45: Al Jathiyah (The Kneeling Down)

More Dramatic Pictures (Surah 44:43-48)

At times the Qur'anic depictions of Hell become very dramatic. These Ayat give a gruesome view of Hell.

> Verily the tree of Zaqqum Will be the food of the Sinful, Like molten brass; it will boil in their insides, Like the boiling of scalding water, Seize ye him and drag him into the midst of the Blazing Fire! Then pour over his head the Penalty of Boiling Water.

Surah 44 and 45 are short but filled with strong warnings to unbelievers that they will be punished, while the believers are promised beautiful young women who will wait upon them in a land of luxury. We do not know if this is meant literally or symbolically. In either case, the Qur'an makes a radical distinction between Paradise and Hell.

Chapter 44

Surah 46: Al Ahqaf (Winding Sand-tracts)

Qur'an Confirms Bible (Surah 46:10)

Here is incontrovertible evidence that the Qur'an does not teach the Tawrat and Zabur were corrupted. Ayat 10 says, "Say: See ye? if be from Allah, and ye reject it, and a witness from among the Children of Israel testifies to its similarity and has believed while ye are arrogant."

Let's think about this. The unbelievers accused Muhammad of forging the Qur'an or speaking under the influence of a demon. In reply, Ayat 10 tells the unbeliever to compare Muhammad's words with the Musa's book. If the Tawrat was corrupted when Ayat 10 was given, Muhammad could not have pointed to the Tawrat as a reliable source of truth. According to the Qur'an, there is no doubt, the Tawrat, Zabur and Injil cannot be corrupted. Anyone who says otherwise is saying that the Qur'an is mistaken to recommend the Earlier Books.[225]

---

[225] Christians and Jews trust the reliability of the Bible based on Allah's faithfulness and on the historical record. Muslims who trust the Qur'an need to reevaluate their attitude toward the Tawrat, Prophets and Injil.

Chapter 45

Surah 47:
Muhammad or Al Qital (The Fighting)

To be Comfortable or Not? (Surah 47:20)

We come in this Surah back to the subject of military service against the unbelievers. Not every follower of Muhammad enjoyed the thought of going into battle.

> Those who believe say, Why is not a Surah sent down? But when a Surah of basic or categorical meaning is revealed, and fighting is mentioned therein, thou wilt see those in whose hearts is a disease looking at thee with a look of one in swoon at the approach of death. But more fitting for them.

This passage goes on to warn those who fall back in fear. They may be comfortable for a time, but it says that in the end the angels will take their souls and beat them on the face and back.

It goes on to say that the believers should never cry out for peace but fight on until they have reached the "uppermost." Perhaps this is one of the reasons that it is customary for Islamic buildings to rise higher than all other buildings. For instance, the House of Saud built a 600-meter-tall (1,972 ft.) clock tower in the heart of Mecca, far taller than Big Ben in London. The symbolism of having the tallest buildings is a powerful reminder that Muslims believe Islam must achieve the uppermost in all things.

Chapter 46

Surah 48: Al Fath (The Victory)

Victory (Surah 48)

Whether we speak of clock towers, economies, armies, mosques or churches, the Qur'an envisions that Islam will advance to victory over all false religion.

> And that He may punish the Hypocrites, men and women, and the Polytheists, men and women, who imagine an evil opinion of Allah. On them is a round of Evil: the Wrath of Allah is on them: He has cursed them and got Hell ready for them: and evil is it for a destination.

In the 21ˢᵗ century many people complain about "imperialist powers." What dark purpose do these powers have? How real is the threat? Is it similar to those mentioned here who have an "evil opinion of Allah?" What does it mean to have an "evil opinion of Allah?"

Chapter 47

Surah 49: Al Hujurat (The Chambers)

Doubt (Surah 49:15)

What should we do with doubt? When does doubt wipe out faith?
The Qur'an warns that real Muslims are those who don't doubt. "Only
those are Believers who have believed in Allah and His Messenger, and
have never since doubted, but have striven with their belongings and
their persons in the Cause of Allah: such are the sincere ones."
Perhaps this means those Muslims who stopped fighting, those who
turned and ran away from the battle. Perhaps it means those who
stopped doing their prayers. But these are only outer behaviors. What
about the heart? It is possible that a person can run into battle and do
their prayers while not truly believing in Allah. It's also possible to
have both faith and doubt at the same time. Feelings and thoughts can
pull us in two directions. At this place where the roads part, do we
walk in fear that Allah will punish any and all doubt or do we say like
the man who cried out to Isa, "Lord, I believe, help my unbelief."[226]

---

[226] Injil, Mark 9:24

Chapter 48

Surah 50: Qaf

Closer than the Jugular Vein (Surah 50:16-17)

My friend wanted me to know that everything I do is being watched. "Allah is closer than our jugular vein. And there is an angel on the right and left, keeping a record of everything we do."

Is Ayat 16 meant to give comfort or fear? I'm not sure. One friend read the verse and said, "This sounds like Allah is warning the unbelievers that he has the power to kill them." Muhammad apparently died from poisoning when he was 62. He said that the poison was cutting at his jugular vein.[227] During battle warriors struck at the jugular hoping to quickly inflict a mortal wound. The jugular is one of the most vulnerable places in the human body.

Ayat 17 leaves me a little confused about whether Allah himself or his

---

[227] "I did not cease to find the effect of the (poisoned) morsel, I took at Khaibar and I suffered several times (from its effect) but now I feel the hour has come of the cutting of my jugular vein." (Ibn Sa'd, Kitab Al-Tabaqat al-Kabir, Volume II, pp. 251-252).

angels are near to humans. Does the Qur'an teach that Allah is extremely close to us or extremely far way in the highest Heaven? Do Muslims believe that anyone will ever reach the presence of Allah himself?

One time I asked another Muslim friend if we would ever meet Allah. "I don't think so. Maybe Muhammad will personally meet Allah, but not regular people." Surah 43:84 says, "It is He Who is Allah in heaven and Allah on earth." We could say this is talking about Allah's authority, not his presence. But in that case he wouldn't be closer than our jugular vein.

Islam is the Tawhid *din* (religion). It teaches that there is no division in Allah. This makes these Ayat interesting, because we discover the presence of Allah existing in more than one kind of place. Allah is on earth and Allah is in Heaven. These are different places, with different conditions. Are we in the same presence of Allah as the angels are in Heaven? Will Paradise have the presence of Allah in the same way as he is on the earth and in the highest Heaven?

The picture of Allah in Heaven and Isa al-Masih on earth helps me understand love manifested. Love folded into himself in three manifestations, Allah can be both in Heaven and on earth. He rules over all in Heaven as the Sovereign and he is present with us on the earth as the Spirit of Allah. He is not limited by time, space or eternity.

Chapter 49

Surah 51: Al Dhariyat (The Winds that Scatter)

Forgiveness (Surah 51:18)

How does guilt feel? Heavy? Dirty? Fearful? Like an alarm, the conscience is designed to tell us that something is wrong. How can we rid ourselves of the feelings of guilt and shame? Some people cry out to Allah for relief. Ayat 18 says, "And in the hours of early dawn, they are praying for Forgiveness."

We pray, but does Allah forgive? What if we sin again, and again? People go into the holy places and pray. They put their shoes back on and return to their sin. Sin and forgiveness and sin. What's the point?

Someone asked a great leader, "Have you ever asked for forgiveness?" He thought a moment, "No, not really, I'm not sure what I've done wrong."

Anyone who says, "I don't have any sin" is a liar. But if we confess our sins, he who is faithful and just will forgive us our sins and cleanse us of all unrighteousness.[228]

Seeking forgiveness isn't a game of chance. Some people think that Allah gives no assurances about forgiveness. He might forgive or he might not. This picture of Allah misses the essential key. Allah forgives based on his promises. He promises to forgive through the sacrifice of the Lamb of Allah. He makes an unbreakable oath that he *will* forgive those who trust in Isa al-Masih. He can't lie.

Our family sat with some friends one afternoon and I told them that Allah keeps his promises. "Allah's promise is more reliable than the warranty papers that come with a new washing machine," I explained, using a simple illustration. "If your new washing machine breaks, you have a document that guarantees the company will repair or replace it. It's 100% certain. In the same way, Allah promises that if we confess our sins, he will forgive them and give us eternal life."

The host's wife became red in the face and raised her voice. "No, that's not right. No one can know if they are fully forgiven and going to Heaven. Where are your warranty papers? Show me!"

"Here," I said, lifting the Injil. "Here is the promise Allah himself has made. Is he less faithful to his promise than the washing machine company? If he says he will do something, he certainly will. There's no doubt."

Forgiven and Forgiving

One day Isa's disciples came to him and said, "Please teach us to pray."

He said, "Pray like this."

> Our Father in Heaven,
> hallowed be your name,
> your kingdom come,

---

[228] Injil, 1 John 1:8

your will be done,
on earth as it is in Heaven.
Give us today our daily bread.
And forgive us our debts,
as we also have forgiven our debtors.
And lead us not into temptation,
but deliver us from the evil one. [229]

If we refuse to forgive someone it means we truly haven't understood Allah's forgiveness.

Late one night a good friend called me. "Have you seen the news?" he asked.

"No," I answered. His tone of voice troubled me deeply.

"You need to check the internet and read what has just happened."

I thanked him for calling and quickly opened a news website. Staring at the screen, I felt my stomach tighten. The news reported that terrorists had brutally murdered three men at an Injil distribution office in the Middle East. The next day we learned the shocking details. Faking interest in learning more about all the Holy Books, several young guys made an appointment to meet some Christian leaders. Two of the Injil office workers had grown up as Muslims and later came to love and trust Isa al-Masih. The third man grew up in secular Europe and became a Christian as a youth. No one may ever know all the reasons why, but the hostile young guys made a plan to attack the three peaceful men.

The terrible day started innocently. A couple of the young guys sat in the office, pretending to act curious about spiritual things.

"Would you like some tea?" the German Christian said, offering some

---

[229] Injil, Matthew 6:9-13

refreshment.

After a few minutes more young men arrived, bringing their total to five. By mid-morning all three of the Christian men had arrived at the office as well. For several minutes the older men tried to answer questions about the Tawrat, al-Masih and the Injil. The five young guys fidgeted nervously and their leader grew angrier in his speech.

Suddenly they violently exploded. The five young guys overpowered their hosts. Knives came into view. They tied the men's wrists and ankles. A couple of the young guys started searching the office. Did they really hope to find guns or drugs? Who knows? They apparently believed many lies about the Christians. There were no guns, only holy books about Allah's love.

The leader of the terrorists screamed at the three Christians lying immobilized on the office floor. "Who sent you?!" Some of the guys stabbed them repeatedly. They moaned and pleaded for their lives.

The torture continued for several minutes. But they weren't done. With three swift motions, someone cut deeply into their necks. We can't describe the gruesome scene.

Outside the office a Christian friend arrived. He couldn't open the locked door, so he quickly called the police. They arrived just minutes later, broke open the door and found all five terrorists still covered with blood. Two of the Christians were dead. An ambulance rushed the third man to the hospital but he died that evening from massive blood loss.

Two of the murdered men left behind wives and the third had a fiancée. Minutes after the police arrived the news media learned about the attack, even before the widows did. With very little information, the two wives waited for hours at the hospital and at home for someone to explain what happened. They both had small children with them, making the long wait terribly painful.

Just a few days later, the victims' families put the bodies of their loved ones into the ground. Through international television, the entire world watched as the widows responded. Would they call for revenge? Would they curse their enemies? Would they hate? One of the ladies stood before the motionless crowd and spoke.

> We wanted to come and live here as Christians. For us this is a very hard time, I have lost my lifelong friend and the children have lost their father. But I know [my husband] died as a martyr in the name of Jesus Christ. His blood was not in vain. For [this land] this is a new start. Jesus said from the cross to the people around him, "Father, forgive them, for they know not what they do" and I want to do the same.[230]

They chose forgiveness, just as Isa did, just as they had been forgiven.

---

[230] James Wright, *The Martyrs of Malatya*, EP Books, Welwyn Garden City, UK, pp 164-165.

Chapter 50

Surahs 52-61

The Shorter Surahs

Much of these final Surah speak about the rewards of Heaven (rivers of water, delicious drinks, beautiful maidens, young servant boys, couches of repose, etc.) and the punishments of sin (fire, black smoke, boiling water, sudden destruction, the Day of Judgment).

Salty and Fresh Waters (Surah 55:19)

"Did you know that the Qur'an accurately predicted there is a boundary between salty and fresh waters? It's what convinced Jacque Cousteau to become a Muslim." My friend was so excited to share the news with me, based on passages like Surah 55:19.

As a boy, I grew up near a great river, one of the largest in the world, similar to the Nile and the Amazon. The river carries rain and flood waters for 3000 kilometers. Eventually all great rivers meet the sea where there is an invisible boundary between the fresh water and salt water. It is true, Allah has put a wall between the sweet and salty waters.

One spring my wife and I flew to the land of Ibrahim and toured it in a rented car. On a bright, sunny morning we bought coffee and breakfast rolls and turned to the north. After a couple of hours our road descended into the deep valley of the Sea of Galilee. We watched fisherman cast their nets into the fresh waters of the sea and we ate falafel for lunch. Then we turned south, driving over the strong fresh waters of the Jordan River. The terrain became very dry in the rugged Jordan River valley. The river's clear waters flow through the fresh-water Sea of Galilee and then southward to the Dead Sea. We followed the river all the way to the edge of the Dead Sea. It is completely and weirdly different. With so much salt dissolved in it, the Dead Sea waters don't allow people to sink. They simply bob up and down on the waters like a piece of cork.

I thought about the two seas and the river connecting them. One is sweet and teems with life. The other full of salt and dead like the grave. In between them the Jordan River patiently flows with clean waters. But no matter how much fresh water it dumps into the Dead Sea, nothing ever changes. An invisible wall remains.

Did the Arabs know about these marvelous facts of nature? Surely they knew about the Nile and the Dead Sea. This is not to say that Allah couldn't reveal something amazing to a messenger of his. It simply means that there is no particular secret about the barriers between salty and fresh waters.

Did Isa Predict Muhammad's Coming? (Surah 61:6)

Often my Muslim friends ask, "Doesn't the Injil talk about Muhammad coming?" We've seen that the word Ahmed, which means *Praised One,* does not appear in the Earlier Books. It does not appear in Hebrew, Greek or Aramaic. Someone could claim the Qur'an is talking about some Ayat lost from the Injil. But how can anything be lost from Allah's Word? Furthermore, one of the Beautiful Names of Allah is the Praised One. Therefore, Isa followers understand his promise of another helper coming after him to be the Spirit of Allah, who is truly praised.

Chapter 51

Surahs 62-70

Jumu'ah Prayer Not Optional (Surah 62:9-11)

What happens in every Muslim community on Jumu'ah? The muezzin gives the call to prayer. All the faithful must wash, go into the mosque and perform their *ibadat* (worship).

But what else happens on Jumu'ah?

"Many of these people aren't good Muslims," my friend said, looking around at people swarming the crowded streets.

"Why," I asked, curious to hear.

"Just watch them on Friday. They don't stop chasing after money and entertainment, not even for a second. No thought of Allah or ibadat (worship). His face showed his disgust.

The Qur'an could not be clearer about Friday prayers. We must read the whole passage.

> O ye who believe! When the call is proclaimed to prayer

on Friday, hasten earnestly to the Remembrance of Allah, and leave off business: that is best for you if ye but knew! And when the Prayer is finished, then may ye disperse through the land, and seek of the Bounty of Allah: and celebrate the Praises of Allah often that ye may prosper. But when they see some bargain or some amusement, they disperse headlong to it, and leave thee standing. Say: The from the Presence of Allah is better than any amusement or bargain! And Allah is the Best to provide.

Does any mumin (believer) have a legitimate excuse for skipping Jumu'ah prayers? Yet in many places Muslims do not attend mosque prayers even once a week. For example, a study showed that in Morocco 54% of Muslims went to Jumu'ah prayers, Egypt 61%, Kazakhstan 10%, Indonesia 72%, Turkey 44%, and Uzbekistan 9%.

As an Isa follower reading the Qur'an, I'm not sure what to think. There are exceptions to Jumu'ah prayer. Doctors and policeman cannot easily pause their work. But many of the people I see on Jumu'ah are simply enjoying a second cup of coffee or smoking a cigarette with a lady friend or a buddy, sharing gossip or discussing the latest business deal.

> The Spirit of Allah is not an angel.

Sure, anyone can point to Christian hypocrisy. I'll be the first to admit that millions of nominal Christians have not entered a church building in decades. If we ask these French or Germans or others why they don't go to worship, they will usually answer honestly that they don't really believe in religion. Is that the same reason so many Muslims don't attend Friday prayers? What does it matter? That's a question I will have to leave with you my friend.

Hypocrites (Surah 63)

Almost as if anticipating our last question, this Surah condemns hypocrites. These people made a very good and convincing show of being Muslims. Muhammad said they were pleasing to the eye but as worthless as a piece of timber propped up.

Allah's Spirit Breathed Into Miriam (Surah 66:12)

Here's another key thought about the Ruhullah. The Spirit of Allah is not an angel.

> And Mary the daughter of Imran, who guarded her chastity; and We breathed into of Our spirit: and she testified to the truth of the words of her Lord and of his Revelations, and was one of the devout.

Chapter 52

Surah 71-78

Read the Qur'an (Surah 73:20)

Years ago a neighbor in our village died. Relatives traveled from far away and neighbors walked over to his house for the funeral ritual. An imam came for a Qur'anic reading. I sat quietly with two dozen others in the family room while the imam chanted the Qur'an in Arabic. No one in the room spoke Arabic, it was a foreign language. The imam continued chanting for many minutes. I looked around the room. People gazed into space and occasionally someone would say, "Bismillah" or "Amin."

Ayat 20 says, "Read ye, therefore, as much of the Qur'an as may be easy." This means to recite the Qur'an audibly.

I am reading the Qur'an with the help of translations. What about my village friends at the funeral? Did they understand anything? They admitted, "We don't understand the imam." How can unintelligible sounds bring their full benefit?

"Wait!" someone says, "Muslims know what's in the Qur'an even if they can't read it themselves." Not always.

Late one night I sat with a large clan in their home. They were devout Muslims and spoke Arabic as their mother tongue. Grandma told me clearly that she doesn't ever shake a man's hand because it is haram.

We talked about Allah and I asked them if they know the story of Nuh and the Flood in the Qur'an. For several embarrassing seconds they looked at me blankly. Grandma said she had never heard of the story. Her young nephew remembered some of the story, so he explained it to her.

The response surprised me. The story of Nuh is one of the most common in the Qur'an, told as often or even more than the story of Musa and the Pharaoh. Yet my hospitable and devout Muslim friends knew almost nothing about it. Is there something more that needs to happen than simply reciting words?

More Penalties and Rewards (Surah 73-78)

These short Surah contrast Muslim believers and unbelievers. The unbelievers at the time of Muhammad rejected his message and many Ayat speak in his defense, declaring that he is neither mad nor possessed. He warned them that they could mock him for a time, but Allah would raise them from the dead and pour out fire upon them in judgment.

Chapter 53

Surahs 79-87

A Blind Man (Surah 80:1-2)

"I was blind, but now I see," the poor beggar answered the stern religious leaders. Born blind, the man had spent his life begging. As a child his parents could do nothing for him. No medicine would heal, no doctor could help.

Then one special day a man walked by. Not just any man. On that day in Kudus two thousand years ago al-Masih passed his way. When Isa looked toward the blind man, he didn't see a pathetic beggar, he saw a man created in Allah's image. Taking some mud made with his own spittle, Isa covered the man's eyes and instructed him to go wash. The man trusted Isa and obeyed. When he washed, behold, he could see.

Only Allah can miraculously heal physically or spiritually blind people. He is the only one who holds the power of life and death in his hand.

In a Tablet (Surah 85:20-21)

It's very important we remember Ayat 21. It says the Qur'an is preserved "in a Tablet." Muhammad says that Jibril spoke the Ayat to him. He said that he could not read or write, so he could not have read a tablet even if he had seen one.

Where is this tablet? This is one of the great puzzles of Islam. If the Tablet is in Heaven, written by Allah, how could it not be eternal alongside Allah? Most Muslims think that the Tablet is eternal, existing forever in Heaven. It is also hard to understand why an eternal book would talk about things like divorce, women's menstruation cycles and the number of wives the prophet could take. Why would Allah record an eternal book about these matters, when these are temporal things? In other words, why would an eternal book of Heavenly things concern itself with historical things? If the Qur'an is eternal, then historical and earthly things are elevated to an eternal and Heavenly level.

Jews and Christians do not believe the Tawrat, Prophets and Injil existed in eternity, but that they were revealed in time through humans who lived over the years. Just as Allah may have *thought* about Adam and Musa and stars and trees before actually creating them in the universe, if he wished, he could have thought about the Earlier Books. But that is different than saying that Adam or the Earlier Books existed forever alongside Allah in Heaven.

Chapter 54

Surahs 88-114

What's Our Problem? (Surah 98:5)

We are approaching the end of the Qur'an. We've seen dozens of Ayat that talk about the People of the Book. These passages leave us with questions. Consider Ayat 5, "And they have been commanded no more than this: to worship Allah, offering Him sincere devotion, being True; to establish regular Prayer; and to practice regular Charity; and that is the Religion right and straight." No mention here of mushrikun, idols, shirk or resisting the Messenger. Yet Surah 98:6 warns that the People of the Book and polytheists who reject the Truth will land in a fiery Hell.

Surah 109 offers a response to non-Muslims.

> O ye that reject Faith! I worship not that which ye worship, Nor will ye worship that which I worship. And I will not worship that which ye have been wont to worship, Nor will ye worship that which I worship. To you be your Way, and to me mine.

In light of Surah 29:46 and other passages, does this Ayat mean that Jews, Christians and Muslims share the same Allah or worship different ones?

Allah Was Not Born (Surah 112)

We come to the end of this journey along the way of the Qur'an. Step by step, Ayat by Ayat, studying from the first word to the last in many languages, this journey has brought us back to the crucial question. Allah is One. So who is Isa al-Masih?

> The only One came from Allah only.

> Say: He is Allah, the One and Only; Allah, the Eternal, Absolute; He begetteth not, nor is He begotten; And there is none like unto Him.

Ayat 3 reads in Arabic لَمْ يَلِدْ وَلَمْ يُولَدْ (He doesn't birth and he isn't born). As we normally understand birth, it means three very important things, 1) two parents, 2) creating a new life, and 3) detachment. When a man and woman make a baby, he or she is a newly created person who never before existed. A baby starts to exist at a definite point in time. After nine months the baby is born and separates from the mother. No longer sharing the same nourishment and drink which passes from the mother's blood to the baby, the new child breaks loose from the mother. They are no longer united but divided. The break is complete. They have separate lives, separate souls and possibly separate destinies.

Looking fully at the Tawrat, Prophets and Injil and having read every word of the Qur'an, I come to Surah 112. When I read "He doesn't birth and he isn't born" (لَمْ يَلِدْ وَلَمْ يُولَدْ), I have a simple response. Yes. Allah has no wife, he does not birth a separate god from himself nor is he born from anyone else. We can say that Allah neither creates another god nor is he created by another god. He is eternally the One and only Allah.[231]

"Aha, congratulations, so you have finally become a Muslim, no longer guilty of shirk!"

But was I ever guilty of shirk? Christians never believed Isa lived inside of Allah during a spiritual "pregnancy", and then he was born, separating into a new and second god. May it never be! Surah 112:3 is correct in this sense, Allah never birthed out a second god and Allah never had a beginning, he never came into existence at birth.

"You are playing games with me now!" I'm sorry if someone feels that way. This matter is far too important for games. Everything pivots on the question of the eternal Word of Allah.

In 325 CE Christian leaders gathered in Nicaea, Anatolia to discuss this puzzle. Who is Masih Isa? They came to an agreement based on careful study of the word *monogenēs* (μονογενής) in the Injil.[232] The concept does not mean birthing a new and separate creature. Instead, *monogenēs* could mean something like the only one always coming forth but never dividing, unity in oneness. Imagine an eternal waterfall begotten from a river, a rainbow eternally begotten from rain or love ever begotten from a loving heart. Isa is the only one eternally coming forth from Allah only. The believers in Nicaea wrote,

I believe in one God, the Father almighty, maker of

---

[231] Prophets, Yeshaya 43:10, "'You are my witnesses,' declares the Lord, 'and my servant whom I have chosen, so that you may know and believe me and understand that I am he. Before me no god was formed, nor will there be one after me.'"

[232] Contrary to common rumors, the Council of Nicaea did not select the "Gospels". To be precise, there is only one Gospel. The writings and letters of the Injil were in place long before Nicaea. The Nicaean Council repudiated Arius, who insisted that Isa was not eternal. "There was a time when He was not."

Heaven and earth and of all things visible and invisible.

And in one Lord Jesus Christ, the only-begotten Son of God, begotten of the Father before all ages, God of God, Light of Light, very God of very God, begotten not made, being of one substance with the Father.[233]

"Why?" my friend asked, sincerely wanting to understand. He continued. "Why go to all that trouble of sending Kalimatullah as a baby? Why face the pains of childhood and the shameful temptations of a young man? Why suffer hateful rejection from his own people? Why die on a Roman cross? Why, why, why...!?"

Muslim believers say, "Allahu Akbar." I too as a child learned from my parents to pray at mealtime, "Allah is great, Allah is good." The Qur'an gets this right.

I looked my friend in the eyes and answered, "Why Isa? Because *Allahu alhabu*. Allah is love."

He relaxed and returned my smile. "I think I'm starting to understand."

---

[233] Nicaean Confession of Faith

Creed of Chalcedon

We, then, following the holy Fathers, all with one consent, teach men to confess one and the same Son, our Lord Jesus Christ, the same perfect in Godhead and also perfect in manhood; truly God and truly man, of a reasonable [rational] soul and body; consubstantial [co-essential] with the Father according to the Godhead, and consubstantial with us according to the Manhood; in all things like unto us, without sin; begotten before all ages of the Father according to the Godhead, and in these latter days, for us and for our salvation, born of the Virgin Mary, the Mother of God, according to the Manhood; one and the same Christ, Son, Lord, Only begotten, to be acknowledged in two natures, inconfusedly, unchangeably, indivisibly, inseparably; the distinction of natures being by no means taken away by the unity, but rather the property of each nature being preserved, and concurring in one Person and one Subsistence, not parted or divided into two persons, but one and the same Son, and only begotten, God the Word, the Lord Jesus Christ; as the prophets from the beginning [have declared] concerning him, and the Lord Jesus Christ himself has taught us, and the Creed of the holy Fathers has handed down to us.

Topical Index

A Blind Man (Surah 80:1-2)

Jews and Christians (People of the Book)
Children of Ibrahim (Surah 2:40)
Muslims, Jews, Christians, Others (Surah 2:62)
Jews, Christians Read the Same Book? (Surah 2:113)
Faith of Ibrahim, Ismail, and Isa (Surah 2:135-6)
Ask the People of the Book (Surah 10:94)
Ask a Christian (Surah 16:43)

Ka'aba
The Ka'aba (Surah 2:127)
Turning the Qiblah (Surah 2:142)

Last Day
Resurrection (Surah 2:259)
The Final Resurrection (Surah 16:38)

Marriage and Family
Divorce and Marriage (Surah 2:221-241)
Orphans and Wives (Surah 4:3)
How Husbands Treat Wives (Surah 4:34)
Kill Not Your Children (Surah 6:151)

Non-Muslims (Kafir)
Religion and Friendship (Surah 3:28)
Dangerous Enemies? (Surah 3:111)
Fake Believers (Surah 9:56)
A New Enemy Introduced (Surah 9:73)
Fake Mosques (Surah 9:107-110)
Hypocrites (Surah 63)

Possessions
Charging Interest on Loans (Surah 2:275)
Fairness to the Needy (Surah 4:9-10)
Slavery (Surah 16:71-76)

Prayer
Praying for Strangers and Enemies (Surah 2:105)

About the Author

After Communism ended in Central Asia in the early 1990s, James Wright and his family made a new home among people of the Tien Shan Mountains. For decades Communists destroyed religious books and taught their people that no Creator exists. In the days of new freedom, many people started studying the holy books hoping to fill their inner spiritual emptiness. Focusing on Allah's miraculous seed who came through Ibrahim's family, Dr. Wright and other teachers have helped people in many countries realize that no matter how deep the darkness, the light of Allah's love is stronger still.

23072386R00178

Made in the USA
Columbia, SC
05 August 2018